MIND TRAINING LIKE THE RAYS OF THE SUN

MIND TRAINING LIKE THE RAYS OF THE SUN

bLo-byong Nyi-ma'i 'Od-zer

by

Nam-kha Pel

Translated by Brian Beresford
&
Edited by Jeremy Russell

LIBRARY OF TIBETAN WORKS AND ARCHIVES

First Print 1992
Reprint 2002

ISBN: 81-85102-71-6

Published by Library of Tibetan Works and Archives, Dharamsala, and printed at Indraprastha Press (CBT), 4 Bahadurshah Zafar Marg, New Delhi-110 002.

CONTENTS

FOREWORD

LTWA is proud to present the translation into English of yet another important text in the Tibetan tradition of mind training, prepared by members of its Translation Bureau. The **Mind Training Like Rays of the Sun** (*bLo sbyong nyi ma'i 'od zer*) was composed by Nam-kha Pel, a close disciple of Je Tsong-kha-pa, and represents one of the most profound transmissions in the genre of mind-training precepts. Its essential meaning is rooted in the practices of the Kadampa masters which were passed down to Tsong-kha-pa. In more recent times, the late Kyabje Yongzin Ling Rinpoche, Senior Tutor to His Holiness the Dalai Lama, and 97th occupant of the Ganden Throne, taught it frequently, especially at the Tibetan monastic universities re-established in South India. Having received this lineage from Kyabje Ling Rinpoche, His Holiness the Dalai Lama has also taught the text on several occasions in Dharamsala, Bodhgaya, and most recently in South India when the young reincarnation of his late tutor was enthroned at his monastery (Drepung Loseling).

The work of translating this text into English began on the recommendation and advice of Kyabje Yongzin Ling Rinpoche. Presenting the photo-offset film copy of the text to me during one of my periodic visits to him he said, 'Gyatsho, as this is my favourite text, I shall present the film of the manuscript to you for your archives, but you must ensure that it will be translated into English for the benefit of those who cannot read or speak Tibetan.' Thus, the project has carried his inspiration and blessings, and the burden of fulfilling it has weighed heavily on me over the years. Now that the translation is complete, I feel enormously relieved. A fresh memory of that event has been awakened in my mind though tinged with a feeling of sadness that he is no longer with us.

The task of translating this text into English was originally begun by Lobsang Choephel Gangchenpa and Alf Vial, who produced a draft version of the Preliminary Teachings section. Then it was taken up by Brian Beresford working with Lobsang Choephel Gangchenpa and Diane Short according to the instruction of Geshey Ngawang Dhargyey. Brian put a great deal of effort into refining the work and presented the manuscript of their translation to me. Finally, Jeremy Russell, working principally with Tsepak Rigzin, has revised and edited it into its present form. My grateful thanks go to all of them for their painstaking efforts and diligence in bringing this important work of translation to completion. I hope it will be of great benefit to the many scholars, students and meditators, as well as to psychologists, scientists and therapists, exploring the healing techniques found in Buddhist teachings and meditation.

Gyatsho Tshering
Director
LTWA

July 1991

PREFACE

It is often said that Tibetan Buddhism encompasses the whole of the Buddha's teaching, because it includes all three vehicles: the low, great and vajra vehicles. Of all the great Indian masters who came to Tibet one of the most influential was Atisha (982-1054 C.E.). He is praised amongst other things for reviving the monastic way of life, but his principal contribution to Tibetan Buddhism was to encourage the integration of the various strands of the Buddha's teaching and their implementation in actual practice.

He composed the *Lamp to the Path of Enlightenment*, which became the prototype for the 'stages of the path' (*lam rim*) literature. It was the first Tibetan text to give a complete survey of the whole path, from the practitioner's first entering into it up to the attainment of enlightenment. Because it is actually a concise text, although practitioners may be concentrating on a particular aspect of practice, by reading or reciting it they can review the whole path and so keep their final aim in perspective. Another feature of this presentation is that it does not simply reveal a step by step approach to enlightenment, but also presents the path in terms of the different kinds of practitioner. There are those of limited capacity, who are primarily concerned with their own good rebirth. There are those of middling capacity, who are aiming for their own liberation from cyclic existence and those of great capacity who are aiming to attain enlightenment for the sake of others.

This stages of the path presentation was absorbed and developed by all schools of Tibetan Buddhism. Je Tsong-khapa's *Great Exposition of the Stages of the Path* is notable for providing one of the largest and most exhaustive commentaries to Atisha's text. An indication of the great value attached to Atisha's *Lamp for the Path* and the integrated approach it presents can be gleaned from its reception in India. When the Tibetans first invited Atisha to visit Tibet, his abbot at Vikramashila monastery was extremely reluctant to let him go. However, after much persuasion he finally agreed on condition that the Tibetans ensured that he returned after a certain time. As it turned out, Atisha was unable to return within the stipulated period, but sent a copy of *Lamp for the Path* in his stead. The Indian scholars at Vikramashila were so impressed with it that they felt they had been compensated, for although they had lost Atisha, if he had not gone to Tibet he would not have written it.

Another of Atisha's major contributions to Tibetan Buddhism was the mind training tradition. He received this from one of his teachers, Dharmamati, a master from Sumatra. This text refers to him as Serlingpa—man from the Golden Isle or man from Sumatra. Of all his many gurus, Atisha regarded this teacher with especial respect and affection because under his tutelage he learned how to actually bring about the awakening mind, which is the key point of the mind training teachings.

To emphasise the value they place on these teachings Tibetans commonly recount the great hardship that Atisha underwent to receive them, stressing the thirteen month voyage and the twelve years he spent with his master in Sumatra. And recalling Atisha's esteem for him the Tibetans in turn hold him in great respect.

The mind training teachings are a great vehicle instruction, because they are mostly concerned with developing the awakening mind, the altruistic mind of enlightenment. They are directed primarily towards the practitioner of great capacity. They deal essentially with transforming our mental attitudes. Firstly, they are concerned with transforming our attitudes towards other beings. One of the greatest obstacles to both ordinary happiness and spiritual progress is self-centredness. While the door to the great vehicle is the aspiration to highest enlightenment based on a deep seated wish to help others in the best possible way, most of us have just the opposite attitude and are predominantly concerned with our own interests. The mind training teachings provide a variety of techniques for subduing this fundamental selfishness and transforming it into concern for others.

One of the special features of the mind training teachings is the advice to transform adversity into advantage. Even though we may have transformed our motivation and outlook in positive ways so that we actually want to help others—through seeing the disadvantages of selfishness and so on—we are continually beset by obstacles and difficulties which prevent our putting our good intentions into practice. So not only do these instructions help us open out towards other beings, but they also help us transform whatever difficulties come our way into something valuable. In addition the mind training teachings help us recognise that our real enemy is our own disturbing emotions. As well as identifying them, they provide us with ways of opposing them directly.

The final set of attitudes that mind training helps us change are those concerned with our view of reality. It is a common Buddhist assertion that our mistaken view of the way things exist is the source of our problems. The great vehicle tenets say that the fault lies in viewing things as being truly existent. The mind training teachings contain the advice to view all phenomena as being like illusions.

His Holiness the Dalai Lama has remarked that these simple but far-reaching techniques of mind training, particularly those with regard to concern for others and turning adversity to advantage, have virtually become part of the Tibetan character. It is just these traits that have enabled them not only to maintain their identity and spirit in the face of great difficulties, but also to rebuild their lives and their culture in exile.

The stages of the path and mind training are two themes of Atisha's presentation of Buddhist doctrine. A third consisted of classic Buddhist scriptures, referred to here as the six original scriptures, including such works as Shāntideva's *Guide to the Bodhisattva's Way of Life* and *Compendium of Trainings*. When the teachings associated with these themes were passed down, from Drom-tön-pa, Atisha's principal disciple and founder of the Kadampa order, the lineages became divided and were preserved in different ways in different traditions. It was not until Je Tsong-kha-pa that these lineages were united in one person once more. He referred to the order that he founded as the new Kadampas—signifying that it emulated the earlier Kadampa masters who followed Atisha. Like them, he emphasised the necessity of practising all the Buddha's teachings, adopting the Kadampa outlook of observing the low vehicle instructions in your external behaviour, the great vehicle in your inner attitude and the tantric path in secret.

The *Mind Training Like the Rays of the Sun* exemplifies Tsong-khapa's presentation of mind training. The author, Nam-kha Pel, as he mentions in his the introduction, received the lineage of the explanation of the *Seven Point Mind Training*, which is the fundamental text here, from various sources including Je Rinpoche, his principal teacher. What is distinctive about this presentation is that he has managed to combine both the mind training instructions as they are recorded in Geshey Che-ka-wa's text the *Seven Point Mind Training* with the pattern of the stages of the path.

Perhaps because these instructions are part of a vibrant oral tradition, there are many slightly different editions of the basic *Seven Point Mind Training* text. This can be seen clearly from a comparison of Nam-kha Pel's edition, which has been extracted and presented here before the text of the *Rays of the Sun* and Thog-me Zang-po's edition which is placed at the end. There are some discrepancies between individual lines, but the most significant difference is that, whereas most of the earlier editions begin with the ultimate awakening mind and a discussion of emptiness, the *Rays of the Sun* version follows the stages of the path pattern and places this section last. Similarly, where the basic text begins simply 'Homage to great compassion' Nam-kha Pel opens his commentary with a prostration to 'the infinitely compassionate spiritual masters' reflecting the first point of the stages of the path approach—the importance of cultivating the spiritual master.

So this edition is unusual in combining the features of the stages of the path and the mind training traditions, two of the major themes of Atisha's presentation of the doctrine. In addition, by also making copious quotations from various classic Indian scriptures it in effect incorporates the third theme too.

In his introduction the author quotes Tsong-kha-pa as pointing out that there appeared to be variations of length and sequence of the basic text, the *Seven Point Mind Training*, and that it would be beneficial if these were clarified. Even though he did so, variations persisted into this century, for we find Pha-bong-kha Rinpoche saying much the same thing in 1935. He had felt for some time that it would be useful to have a definitive edition of the *Seven Point Mind Training*. His consequent version was drawn from sources already accepted as belonging to the Gelug tradition. Found among Trijang Rinpoche's Miscellaneous Works, it is indeed useful because it is clearly laid out under simple headings and includes full ennumerated lists of the commitments and precepts of the practice of mind training. For this reason it has also been included here at the end of the book.

Now, whatever can be said about his text, little is known about the author. Hortön Nam-kha Pel was a direct disciple of Je Tsong-kha-pa and in the latter's Collected Works Nam-kha Pel-sang's name is often mentioned as the scribe. This has lead to the suggestion that *Mind Training Like the Rays of the Sun* may be something like a transcription of Tsong-kha-pa's oral explanation. If this were so it would be valuable for representing how he actually taught as opposed to how he wrote, of which there is ample evidence.

It happens that among Tsong-kha-pa's Collected Works there are two letters to Nam-kha Pel. In one of them Je Rinpoche thanks him for a present he has sent and addresses him as 'one with clear intelligence whose faith is firm'. He praises his generosity and he comments that he has heard much, from which we can assume that he has listened to many of Je

Rinpoche's teachings. It seems that Nam-kha Pel had sent him a statue of a Bodhisattva and a text of the Guhyasamaja Tantra beautifully wrapped in orange coloured banners. Je Rinpoche comments that it was delivered intact and thanks him for his letter which was full of good and agreeable words. He goes on to remark, 'You say that what I taught you before was useful and that you are practising what I taught. You request me for more teachings, but I have no more to teach you than what I taught before, there's nothing better than that. However, if you listen with respect and interest again and again to what is taught well, then just as drops of water falling repeatedly on a rock will eventually wear out a channel, so you will derive benefit.'

There is a second letter the gist of which is that Je Rinpoche says, 'In reply to the letter sent by the intelligent novice monk, the fully ordained monk Lobsang Drakpa, who has heard a great deal, and who is getting rid of negative traits, has this to say: You say you have pure thoughts, this is good, your mind is pure.' What we can conclude is that Je Rinpoche treated Nam-kha Pel with affection and praised him for his practice.

His Holiness the Dalai Lama mentioned when he taught the *Mind Training Like the Rays of the Sun* in Dharamsala in 1985 that he had received the explanation and transmission of this text from his Senior Tutor, the precious Ganden Throne-holder, Yongzin Ling Rinpoche. He in turn had received it from an Amdo lama called Minyak Rinpoche, a very good lama, who was an old monk with a huge red nose. His Holiness said that he received it from Yongzin Ling Rinpoche after they had arrived in India. It was Ling Rinpoche's favourite mind training text and he was responsible for popularising it. He taught it a couple of times at the re-established monasteries in South India and once here in Dharamsala. His Holiness went on to say that the basic theme of the text is the generation of an awakening mind, a greater concern for others than for yourself, which is the central pillar of the great vehicle teaching. So, this mind training represents the very core of the great vehicle practitioner's practice. Not only does it provide an understanding of the points to be followed, but it describes how to actually apply them.

Although Brian Beresford and others had already translated the majority of this work, there were still some folios missing so it was not totally complete. As a result it was again thoroughly revised and edited. I would like to acknowledge a number of people who helped me in doing this. The members of the LTWA's Translation Bureau, specifically Tsepak Rigzin, Tenzin Dorje, and Thubten Tashi assisted in completing and revising the translation. Ven. Yelo Tulku and Lobsang Shastri of the Library's manuscript room offered patient bibliographical help. In particular I wish to thank Geshey Sonam Rinchen and Ruth Sonam for taking the time to unravel some of the knotty problems in the presentation of the ultimate awakening mind section. Finally, thanks to LTWA's Director, Mr Gyatsho Tshering, for his fathomless patience and long-standing interest in the project.

July 1991 Jeremy Russell

Part One

INTRODUCTION and PRELIMINARY TEACHINGS

THE SEVEN POINT MIND TRAINING

Homage to great compassion.
The essence of this nectar of secret instruction
Is transmitted from the master from Sumatra (Ser-ling-pa).

You should understand the significance of this instruction
As like a diamond, the sun and a medicinal tree.
This time of the five degenerations will then be transformed
Into the path to the fully awakened state.

First, train in the preliminaries.

Banish the one to blame for everything,
Meditate on the great kindness of all beings.

Practise a combination of giving and taking.
Giving and taking should be practised alternately
And you should begin by taking from yourself.
These two should be made to ride on the breath.
Concerning the three objects, three poisons and three virtues
The instruction to be followed, in brief,
Is to take these words to heart in all activities.

When the environment and its inhabitants overflow with
unwholesomeness,
Transform adverse circumstances into the path to
enlightenment.
Apply meditation immediately at every opportunity,
The supreme method is accompanied by the four practices.

Train in the five powers.
The five powers themselves are the great vehicle's

Precept on the transference of consciousness,
Cultivate these paths of practice.

Integrate all the teachings into one thought,
Primary importance should be given to the two witnesses,
Constantly cultivate only a peaceful mind.
The measure of a trained mind is that it has turned away,
There are five great marks of a trained mind.
The trained (mind) retains control even when distracted.

Always train in the three general points,
Engage vigorously in forceful cultivation and abandonment,
Subjugate all the reasons (for selfishness).
Train consistently to deal with difficult situations,
Don't rely on other conditions.

Transform your attitude, but maintain your natural behaviour
Don't speak of (others') incomplete qualities,
Don't concern yourself with others' business,
Give up every hope of reward.

Avoid poisonous food,
Don't maintain inverted loyalty,
Don't make malicious banter,
Don't wait in ambush,
Don't strike at the vital point,
Don't place the load of a horse on a pony,
Don't sprint to win the race,
Don't turn gods into devils,
Don't seek others' misery as a means to happiness.

Every yoga should be performed as one.
There are two activities at both beginning and end,
Train first in the easier practices.
Whichever occurs be patient with both,
Guard both at the cost of your life.
Train in the three difficulties,

Transform everything into the great vehicle path,
Value an encompassing and far reaching practice,
Seek for the three principal causes,
Purify the coarser ones first,
Practise that which is more effective,
Don't let three factors weaken,
Never be parted from the three possessions.
If you relapse, meditate on it as the antidote.
Engage in the principal practices right now,
In future, always put on armour.

Don't apply a wrong understanding,
Don't be sporadic,
Practise unflinchingly,
Release investigation and analysis,
Don't be boastful,
Don't be short-tempered,
Don't make a short-lived attempt,
Don't expect gratitude.

When stability has been attained, impart the secret teaching:
Consider all phenomena as like dreams,
Examine the nature of unborn awareness.
The remedy itself is released in its own place,
Place the essence of the path on the nature of the basis of all.
In between meditation sessions, be like a conjuror -or-
In the period between sessions be a creator of illusions.

THE AUTHOR'S HOMAGE AND REQUEST

At all times I take refuge in, and prostrate at the feet of the sublime and infinitely compassionate spiritual masters.
Out of their immense love, may they care for me in every moment of my life.

A PRAYER OF DEVOTION

Arising from the source of love and compassion
The ship of the awakening mind is well launched:
Above it billow the great sails of the six perfections and the four ways of amassing disciples
Which are driven by the wind of enthusiastic effort that never slackens;
Perfectly it carries embodied beings across the ocean of cyclic existence
Landing them on the wish-fulfilling jewel island of omniscience.
I prostrate, placing my head at the feet of the leaders of the spiritual lineage:
The Subduer who is our supreme navigator, the powerful (Buddha Shākyamuni);
Maitreya and his (spiritual followers) Asaṅga, Vasubhandu and Vidyakokila;
Mañjushrī and (his followers) Nāgārjuna and the supreme wise saint Shāntideva
The ruler of the Golden Isle (of Sumatra) and (his disciple) the noble Atīsha;
And (his Tibetan disciple) Drom-tön-pa[1] and his three spiritual brothers (Po-to-wa, Phu-chung-wa and Chen-nga-wa)[2]

I prostrate at the feet of the great emanation of Mañjushrī,

Tsong-kha-pa, the second conqueror of these degenerate times,
Who propounded the individual spiritual paths
Of these great pioneers with extreme lucidity and coherence.
Supreme among all his wonderful teachings
Are the means for activating the awakening mind.
I shall expound his perfect teaching with absolute accuracy;
Those fortunate to follow the way of the great vehicle should
pay close attention for true appreciation.

This exceptional oral transmission of great vehicle mind training, an instruction for cultivating the precious awakening mind of *bodhichitta*[3] will be explained in two main parts: an introduction giving an historical account of the lineage of these teachings including their unique qualities which will encourage the intelligent to appreciate them with genuine interest; and the explanation of the actual teaching, a most royal instruction.

INTRODUCTION

The background to these teachings can be presented in two ways. Firstly, by relating the common greatness of the teaching and the historical account of the lineage, the authenticity of the teaching is clarified. Secondly, through expressing the particular eminence of the instruction with regard to its extraordinary function, a respect and appreciation of the spiritual value of the instruction will be created.

An Historical Account of the Teaching

The text says,

> *The essence of this nectar of secret instruction*
> *Is transmitted from the master from Sumatra (Ser-ling-pa)*

In general, the eighty-four thousand collections of Buddhist teachings or the three progressive turnings of the wheel of the doctrine taught by the Buddha can all be condensed into two intentions: to put an end to all types of mental distortion with regard to the 'I' or the misconception of self[4] and thereby to acquaint ourselves with an altruistic attitude through which we take responsibility for the welfare of others. The former theme was expounded in the spiritual paths of the two vehicles of the Hearers and the Solitary Realisers. This was expressed in the corpus of the low vehicle teachings for the benefit of those belonging to those categories. The theme of the latter involves the causal relationship between the great vehicle teachings in the general discourses and the secret teachings of tantra. Here, for those who are fortunate, are explained the teachings on the practice for cultivating the awakening mind. It is the entrance into the practices of the great vehicle and the means for attaining the fully awakened state of complete omniscience.

Moreover, all the teachings of Buddha, the Transcendent Subduer, pertaining to activating the awakening mind are found in the three systems introduced by the great pioneers. All these are sacred and ultimately supreme spiritual nectar capable of revealing the nonabiding state transcending sorrow, the nirvana which destroys the eighty-four thousand kinds of disturbing emotions and their creations, even all such misery as birth, ageing, sickness and death.

In general, the term 'nectar' in the text refers to the elixir which provides immortality. So it is here, just as a proficient doctor when diagnosing an illness prescribes a medicine that can relieve the patient of his sickness and even prevent his death, so the Perfection of Wisdom Sutras tell of the finest type of medicine, even the smell of which is said to drive away the most venomous of snakes. These teachings constitute the universal panacea that can provide true immortality. So, by developing the intention to realise the attainments of the Hearers and the Solitary Realisers we can familiarise ourselves with all aspects of that spiritual path, which can result in the attainment of the state free from birth, ageing, sickness and death. Yet, developing the intention to realise the unsurpassable fully awakened state of being, the ultimate goal of existence, together with total acquaintance with the entire scope of its spiritual path, can result in the omniscient state of full enlightenment, the state of one who has Gone Beyond to Thusness, the state of a Tathagata. This is the point of complete cessation of every disturbing emotion, which even the worthy saints, the Arhats[5] among the Hearers and Solitary Realisers and even the great Bodhisattvas, the Bodhisattvas on the pure stages, have not completely eliminated.

The precious awakening mind is the supreme essence of any spiritual endeavour, the nectar providing the state of immortality. The exalted Buddhist saint from Sumatra was a man who held the lineages of the complete spiritual systems of the great pioneers, (such as Nāgārjuna, Asaṅga, and Shāntideva) much like the point of confluence of three great rivers. He imparted these teachings to the great Indian pandit Atīsha (982-1054 C.E.) in a way that was like the filling of one vase from another that was identical. Atīsha had innumerable disciples from India, Kashmir, Urgyan, Nepal and Tibet, all of whom were scholars and accomplished meditators. From among them all it was the Tibetan Drom-tön-pa (1005-64), also known as Gyal-wai-jung-nae[6], and who was prophesied (to Atīsha before he went to Tibet by his divine ally), the goddess Ārya Tāra, who became the major holder of his spiritual lineages, extending the noble deeds of the master (to a multitude of followers throughout the centuries).

Drom-tön-pa had as many realised disciples as the population of the land of Urgyen[7], north-west of Ra-treng[8]. In particular, there were the 'Three Noble Brothers' (Po-to-wa, Phu-chung-wa and Chen-nga-wa) who elucidated his teaching in an unbroken transmission of 'whispered instruction', through which they imparted the very essence of their master's words. The most renowned of these three was the spiritual friend, Geshey[9] Po-to-wa (1031-1106), an incarnation of the (Buddha's disciple), the Exalted Elder Angaja (one of the sixteen Arhats). Receiving the entire scriptural teaching and hidden verbal transmission of both sutra and tantra from Drom-tön-pa, Po-to-wa was very successful in his religious activity. He undertook a thorough study of and then taught the Six Original Scriptures[10]: *Ornament for the Great Vehicle Sutras* by Asaṅga/Maitreya; *Spiritual Stages of Bodhisattvas* by Asaṅga; *Birth Stories* by Aryashūra; *Special Verses Collected by Topic* compiled by Dharmatrata; *Compendium of Trainings* and *Guide to the Bodhisattva's Way of Life* by Shāntideva.

He fulfilled his faith in the Buddha by maintaining the precious jewel of the awakening mind as the very heart of his practice, teaching about it and putting it into practice. He had over two thousand disciples involved in the pursuit of liberation. From among those the most prominent were Lang and Nyö from Nyal, Ram and Nang from Tsang, Ja and Phag from Kham, 'Be and Rog from Dolpo, Lang and Shar whose fame was equal to the sun and moon in the Central Province of U, Geshey Drab-pa, Geshey Ding-pa, the great Geshey Drag-kar, and many others.[11]

The great Zhan-tön Sha-ra-wa[12] (1070-1141) received the entire teaching, both scriptural and verbal, and was considered the one responsible for maintaining the transmission of his master's deeds. He conducted many discourses on the Six Original Scriptures and other teachings, speaking to around two thousand eight hundred monks. His most outstanding disciples were popularly known as the Four Sons. Chö-lung Ku-sheg was responsible for willing service, the great Tab-ka-wa was responsible for explaining the teaching, Nyi-mel-dul-wa-dzin-pa was responsible for blessing and inspiring the holders of monastic discipline and the great Che-ka-wa[13] (1101-1175) was to be responsible for transmitting the teachings on the awakening mind.

The great Geshey Che-ka-wa first received such teachings from Nyel-chag-zhing-pa[14] on the *Eight Verses for Training the Mind*, a text by Lang-ri-tang-pa (1054-1123). This had the effect of arousing his faith and interest in the Kadampa teachings and he set out for Lhasa with the intention of seeking teachings on mind training in greater detail. Some of his worthy friends suggested that since a master of the great vehicle should be high in the esteem of others, like the sun and moon, it would be best for him to approach the great Sha-ra-wa and Ja-yul-wa directly. Accordingly, he went to the House of Zho in Lhasa where Sha-ra-wa was staying. When he arrived the master was teaching about the spiritual levels of the low vehicle's Hearers. After listening to him, however, Che-ka-wa felt no inspiration at all, and instead became despondent and confused. In despair he resigned himself to fulfilling his quest elsewhere if, when asked directly, Sha-ra-wa revealed that he did not hold the tradition of teachings on mind training, or that they could not be taken to heart in practice.

The next day, after the lunch offering had been made to the monastic community, while the master was circumambulating a stupa, the reliquary monument to the Buddha mind, Che-ka-wa approached him. Spreading a cloth on a prominent ledge he said, 'Will you please sit down? I have something I would like to discuss with you.'

The master replied, 'Ah, teacher, what is it that you haven't understood? I made everything absolutely clear when I sat on the religious throne.'

Che-ka-wa then produced the *Eight Verses for Training the Mind* by Lang-ri-tang-pa and said, 'I was wondering whether you hold the tradition of this teaching? I've found that it often helps my useless self just a little when all my thoughts run wild, or in times of hardship when I'm unable to find shelter, or when I'm scorned or cast out by others. Yet I also find that there seem to be a few occasions when it is not so appropriate to practise. Therefore, I humbly ask you whether it is really worth putting into practice or not? Will the final result of such practice be actually to lead one to the fully awakened state or not?'

Geshey Sha-ra-wa first completed counting the round of his bodhi-seed rosary before rolling it up, composing himself and preparing his reply. 'Ah, teacher, there is no question whether this practice is appropriate or not. If you have no desire for the one and only state of a fully awakened being, you can leave it aside. However, should you yearn for such a state, it is impossible to attain it without directly entering this spiritual path.'

'Very well, as this is a Buddhist tradition, I am interested to know where the definitive reference for this practice and experience may be found. Since a religious quotation requires a scriptural reference, do you recollect where it might be?'

'Who would not recognise it as from the impeccable work of the truly exalted master Nāgārjuna? It comes from his *Precious Garland (of Advice for a King)*, (where it says),

> 'May their evil bear fruit for me
> May all my virtue bear fruit for others.'

'O, gentle sir, I have such deep faith in that teaching.

Please, out of your kindness, take me under your guidance.'

The master replied, 'Then try to stay. The conditions here will sustain you.'

Che-kha-wa then asked, 'Why didn't you give even the slightest hint of this teaching to the assembly during your discourse before?'

To which the master responded, 'Oh, there was no point in telling them of it. They're not really able to appreciate the full value of this teaching and training.'

After making three prostrations, Che-kha-wa departed and sought out the exact verse in a copy of the *Precious Garland*, which he found among his landlord's scriptures. Then, relying completely on the *Precious Garland*, he spent the next two years at the House of Zho, during which he dedicated himself completely to that text to the exclusion of all others. In this way he perceived the (nature of) appearances as Nāgārjuna had described them, such that his creation of conceptual thoughts decreased. He then spent six years at Gye-gong and four years at Shar-wa. Altogether he spent fourteen years at the feet of his master, making himself familiar with the teaching and gaining experience of purification. Once this experience had arisen he said that it was so worthwhile that even if he had had to sell all his land and cattle for gold to pay for the teaching it would not have mattered, nor would he have minded being forced to sleep in the muck of the stables in order to receive them.

The great Che-kha-wa's disciples included over nine hundred monks who were devoted to the cause of liberation. Among them was the yogi Jang-seng of Dro-sa, the meditator Jang-ye from Ren-tsa-rab, Gen-pa-ton-dar of Ba-lam, the all-knowing master Lho-pa, Gya-pang Sa-thang-pa, the great teacher Ram-pa Lha-ding-pa, the unequalled master Gyal-wa-se,[15] and many others, who became both spiritual protectors and refuge for a vast number of beings. In particular, Se-chil-bu (1121-89) spent twenty-one years at his side, just like a body and its shadow, during which time he received the entire transmission of scriptural and oral teaching, in such a way that he acquired a complete understanding as if the contents of one vase had been poured out to fill another just like it. Se-chil-bu gave the teachings on cultivating the awakening mind to Lha-chen-po Lung-gi-wang-chug[16] (1158-1232) his nephew, and others, from whom the lineage descends. I had the great fortune to receive the complete transmission of the teachings from the great spiritual being possessing inconceivable compassion and power, Sha-kya So-nam Gyel-tsen Pel-zang-po[17] (1312-75).

I received the lineages of Ram-pa Lha-ding-pa and the great explanation of the Seven Point (Mind Training) by the great hero and Bodhisattva of these degenerate times, the son of the Conquerors, Thog-me Zang-po[18], from his disciple, the great translator, Kyab-chog Pal-zang-po[19]

I received Lha-ding-pa's Seven Points in the form of an experiential explanation from the supreme navigatòr and protector of this world and the gods, the emanation of Mañjushrī, the easterner, the omniscient Tsong-kha-pa (1357-1419), who said,

'Of the many individual lineages of training in the awakening mind of the great pioneers, this tradition of Che-kha-wa's seems to be an instruction derived from the exalted Shāntideva's text, therefore it must be explained according to that.

There seem to be variations in the length and sequence of the text, so if it were explained in good order it would be an instruction that pleases the wise. I shall therefore explain it accordingly.'

THE UNIQUE FEATURES, VALUE AND EXTRAORDINARY FUNCTION OF THIS SECRET INSTRUCTION

So that others may come to respect and appreciate this oral teaching, let me commend it, pointing out some of its unique features. The text says,

You should understand the significance of this instruction
As like a diamond, the sun and a medicinal tree.

This time of the five degenerations will then be transformed
Into the path to the fully awakened state.

There is no need to mention the extent to which a diamond is able to satisfy desire and dispel poverty, for even a fragment of one surpasses all other jewels, retaining the name diamond and averting impoverishment. Similarly, knowing even a small part of this teaching on mind training, which leads to the activation of the awakening mind, means that one retains the name of 'awakening warrior', a bodhisattva, while at the same time excelling the crowned masters of both the Hearers, and the Solitary Realisers, as well as completely dispelling the poverty of cyclic existence. This being so, what need is there to mention what a full comprehension of the whole teaching on mind training would mean in terms of its qualities and value.

There is no place or time when darkness directly covers the sun and there is no darkness anywhere when the sun is shining. Similarly, there is no need to mention the extent to which the instructions for training in the awakening mind, described below, eliminate the darkness of the mind, for by knowing just one part of this teaching you can eliminate the self-centred attitude induced by the ignorance of misconceiving the self and the darkness of the primary and secondary disturbing emotions. In the case of a medicinal plant which has the power to cure the 424 diseases, even its parts such as its roots, fruits, leaves, flowers and branches also have such power. Similarly, there is no need to mention how, if you understand the teachings on mind training, they will uproot the chronic disease of the 84,000 disturbing emotions, because understanding but one part of this teaching will serve as the most perfect remedy for all these ailments.

Buddha Shākyamuni descended particularly at a time when the five degenerations were at their worst and beings' thoughts were preoccupied by disturbing emotions and their actions unwholesome, accumulating only negativity. When misfortune falls upon others they perversely rejoice and are jealous when hearing of others' well-being, which gives rise to pain in their hearts. Cyclic existence is filled with those whose actions of body, speech and mind are employed only in harming others, so at this time the protectors of the doctrine, the gods and nagas[20] who support right actions have gone to other worlds to support the doctrine and the four classes of Buddha's disciples. On the other hand all hostile human and non-human beings who favour wrong actions increase their activities, creating various calamities, particularly against those who follow the theory and practice of the holy doctrine. It is therefore all the more important that such people implement the teaching explained in this text, otherwise they will be unable to continue their practice of the doctrine.

If we enter the gateway of this practice, we will be able to transform unfavourable into favourable circumstances. This is the action of a wise man. This teaching provides the power to defeat all adversaries and overcome all obstacles on the path. If we travel in this way, the way of development and meditation, we can see our bodies as the Blissful Pure Land. Then unfavourable circumstances, whether internal or external, will neither cause misery nor upset the mind, but will be transformed into factors conducive to happiness. This is known as the undisturbed worldly realm and even a great heap of fire-like afflictions, whether physical or mental, will not move or disturb the mind. This is called the city of the source of happiness and is the point of attaining the single-pointed meditation capable of easily following all doctrines. A little practice at this time when the five degenerations arise and we are overwhelmed by both internal and external impediments will be more swiftly effective than accumulating merits for aeons in a pure land. Such is the special method for transforming bad times into good ones, an explanation of which follows below.

Part Two

EXPLANATION OF THE TEACHING

CONTEMPLATION OF THE PRELIMINARY TEACHINGS

The text says,

> *First, train in the preliminaries*

This involves contemplating the significance and rarity of life as a free and fortunate human being, contemplating impermanence and death, which leads to the realization that our lives can end at any time, and thinking about the causes and results of actions and the vicious nature of cyclic existence. From these basic practices up to the training in the ultimate awakening mind, the practice can be divided into two: the actual meditation session, and the period between sessions. The actual session is also divided into three—preparation, meditation and behaviour.

Firstly, as the life-story of guru Dharmamāti of Sumatra shows, we should decorate the place, arrange representations of the Three Jewels (the Buddha, the Fully Awakened Being, his Doctrine and the Spiritual Community), offer a mandala (representing the world system) and complete the six kinds of conduct up to the request that the three great purposes (of self, others and both) shall be fulfilled.

Secondly, during the actual meditation session, we should reflect that throughout beginningless time we have been under the power of the mind and the mind in turn has been overcome by disturbing emotions. These disturbing emotions are what have given rise to the actions that are the root of cyclic existence. From these have arisen the various types of sufferings that we experience in the round of existence. To turn away from such tendencies we must try to develop an independent, controlled and workable mind that will stay where it is put or go where it is sent. To acquire such a state of mind it is necessary to focus on the specific subject of meditation without being distracted by either laxity or excitement. These meditations should follow the given order and, except for the training in the perfection of concentration, they are all analytical meditations.

Thirdly, in conclusion, we should make perfect prayers such as the *Prayer of Good Conduct*, and so forth. We should practise in this way three times during the day and three times during the night.

During meditation sessions the senses should be controlled, mental alertness and introspection maintained and a balanced diet observed. Efforts should be made to become an unsleeping yogi and you should know how to use the period of sleep to develop calm abiding and special insight as taught by the exalted Asaṅga.

LIFE AS A FREE AND FORTUNATE HUMAN BEING

The nature of life as a free and fortunate human being is freedom from the eight states without leisure and possession of the ten beneficial circumstances. The eight states with no leisure are given in the *Friendly Letter*,

> Being born as one holding wrong views, as an animal,
> A hungry ghost, or a hell-being,
> In a place where the Buddha's word does not prevail,
> As a barbarian in remote regions, stupid and dumb,
>
> Or as a long living god are the eight
> States without leisure.
> Having found the opportunity of freedom from them,
> Exert yourself to turn away birth.

The eight states without leisure fall into two categories, four pertaining to human and four to inhuman life.

The ten beneficial circumstances or opportunities are also

divided into two, five personal opportunities: being born as a human being, in a central place, with sound sense organs, not holding wrong views and having faith in the Buddha's doctrine; and five circumstantial opportunities: the appearance of a Buddha and his having given teaching, the prevalence of the doctrine and its followers and the presence of sincere patrons and benefactors. It is important to think over these ten unique opportunities.

The general basis for attaining ultimate definite goodness is birth as a human being, but of such births among the three continents, birth as a human being in the southern continent[21] is praised in all the sutras and tantras as the best working basis for attaining liberation. The master Ashvaghosha says,

> When you have obtained (a human life) with the potential
> To go beyond cyclic existence,
> The most excellent potential of the awakening mind,
> More precious than a wish-granting jewel,
> What wise man
> Would not make it fruitful?

The *Guide to the Bodhisattva's Way of Life* says,

> So if, when I have found such leisure as this
> I do not attune myself to what is wholesome,
> There could be no greater deception
> And no greater folly.
>
> And if, having understood this,
> I still continue to be slothful,
> When the hour of death arrives
> Tremendous grief will rear its head.
>
> Then if my body blazes for a long time
> In the unbearable flames of hell,
> Inevitably my mind will be tormented
> By fires of unendurable remorse.

Having found by chance
This beneficial state so hard to find,
If now while able to discriminate
I am once again led into the hells,

Then it is as though I were mindless,
Like one hypnotised by a spell,
Not even knowing what causes my confusion,
Or what is dwelling inside me.

Again the great Ashvaghoṣha says,

Whoever is rich in virtue,
Has accumulated it over countless aeons,
But he who because of delusion
Does not gather such treasure in this life
Will in his lives to come
Be imprisoned in a house of woe,
Like a merchant returning empty-handed
From the island of jewels.
Without the path of ten virtues
There is no way to obtain a human birth,
Without which there is no happiness
And only suffering remains.
Not to follow such a path
Is an act of supreme stupidity.

Thinking about this will give rise to a wish to take the essence of this teaching to heart. As the *Guide to the Bodhisattva's Way of Life* says,

Now, having paid my body its wages,
I shall turn my life to something meaningful.

And,

Relying on the boat of a human body,
Free yourself from the great river of pain.
As it is hard to find this boat again,
This is no time to sleep, you fool.

Po-to-wa tells the following stories in his *Teachings by Example*,

> Once a man was ploughing his field when he turned up an earth-worm. To his amazement, the red worm stood on end and prostrated to a nearby image of the Buddha. It is equally rare for someone like us, just coming up from a bad state of rebirth, to turn up as a human being and do something positive and spiritually beneficial.
>
> On another occasion a man with no legs was resting on the edge of a short drop. He lost his balance and, falling off, landed on the back of a wild ass beneath. The startled beast ran off at a gallop and the man hung on for dear life, shouting with glee, 'If I don't enjoy it now, when else will a cripple like me get the chance to ride on an ass?' Likewise, we should see how rare our lives are and take joyful advantage of them.
>
> Once a man from Tsang came to Lhasa. He had never eaten fish before, so when he then got the chance he gorged himself on this rare treat. Naturally, it made him sick, but as he was about to vomit he tied a rope round his neck so as not to waste any of what he had eaten. We should be as unwilling to waste even a moment of our precious human lives.
>
> On an occasion when his family were able to enjoy a rare delicacy, sweet buttered barley flour, a small boy, hoping to get an extra helping, held his hands out in front of him after hiding his share behind his back, where a dog ate it, leaving him none. We should take whatever opportunities we have to put the teachings into practice, rather than simply trying to collect more.

From the above we can understand the importance of seeking a birth with high status. The cause of birth with the high status of a human being or god is familiarity with the three types of ethics and life as a human being of this world is an excellent basis for this.

As it is said,

> When you have obtained birth as a human of this world,
> Which is so difficult to obtain,
> You should practise virtue with the utmost effort.

Contemplation of the rarity of such a human life is done in two parts: according to the difficulty of obtaining the cause and according to the difficulty of obtaining the result.

CONTEMPLATION OF THE RARITY OF SUCH A HUMAN LIFE ACCORDING TO THE DIFFICULTY OF OBTAINING THE CAUSE

The *Four Hundred Verses* says,

> When the majority of human beings
> Are involved in unholy activities,
> The majority of ordinary people
> Will certainly go to bad rebirths.

Even beings with high status are continually engaged in unwholesome activities and rarely do they resolve to avoid them in the future. Thus, many of them go to bad rebirths and find it very hard to obtain a birth with high status. As the *Guide to the Bodhisattva's Way of Life* says,

> If my behaviour is like this
> I shall not win a human body again,
> And if this human form is not attained
> There will be solely evil and no virtue.

And the *Friendly Letter* says,

> For an animal to obtain birth as a human being
> Is more difficult than for a blind turtle
> To put its neck through a hole in a yoke adrift in the great ocean

So make your life meaningful, O king, by practising the holy teachings.

Even more stupid than one who vomits
Into a bejewelled golden vessel
Is one who, born as a human being,
Indulges in unwholesome deeds.

CONTEMPLATION OF THE RARITY OF FINDING SUCH A HUMAN LIFE ACCORDING TO THE DIFFICULTY OF OBTAINING THE RESULT

In general, the beings in the three bad rebirths are many, but those with high status are few. Among those with high status in particular it is rare to find those who are free from the eight states without leisure. Moreover, even amongst those who have found freedom and opportunity, those who are inclined towards the holy doctrine are as numerous as stars in the daytime. Appreciating that the precious state of leisure and opportunity, that we have found on this occasion, is very meaningful and difficult to find, we must find the ways and means to generate the wish to extract its essence. In a broad sense, extracting the essence means to practise the holy doctrine. This is because we want happiness and dislike suffering. If any doubt arises about our ability to practise the doctrine, reflect on such external conditions as the presence of spiritual friends of the great vehicle and the opportunities for meeting them, and the internal condition of possessing this free and fortunate body as a basis. If you think of postponing your practice until future lives, remember that it is hard to find such leisure and opportunity again. If you think of putting off your practice for some months or years, this is also mistaken, because although death is assured its time is uncertain. Among the ways of taking the essence, familiarizing yourself with the awakening mind is the principal and most excellent practice, and to do that you should engage in the preliminaries for training in the awakening mind.

HOW TO THINK ABOUT THE BREVITY OF THIS LIFE, DEATH AND IMPERMANENCE

We should think about how being unmindful of death is the main cause of the whole heap of mistakes performed in this and future lives and how familiarity with death and impermanence is advantageous, the sole means for achieving everything excellent in this and future lives.

The fear of being separated from your body, possessions and relatives of this life to which you are attached, caused by thinking about death, is not the fear intended here for that is the fear of one who has no understanding of the path. What is this about? Everything that is born from a union (of parents) due to the forces of action and disturbing emotions is bound to die, and although you may fear it it cannot be avoided. Moreover, until we have accomplished the purpose of our future lives we will continue to fear death. If you think about that and realize it at the time of death you will have no fear.

The actual ways to think about death are to reflect on the inevitability of death, the uncertainty of the time of death, and that only the doctrine can help at the time of death.

THE INEVITABILITY OF DEATH

Death is certain to come, because no one who has a body can avoid dying. In the *Special Verses Collected by Topic* it says,

> If Buddhas, Solitary Realisers
> And Hearers
> Have all abandoned their bodies,
> What can be said about ordinary beings.

In whatever land you may live, you can never avoid death. The same text says,

> Wherever you live you are not immune to death,
> Neither on the earth in any direction,

Nor in space, nor within the ocean,
Nor if you were to hide amidst the mountains.

Even taking rebirth does not avert death. The same text says,

The wise have understood that those of the past
And those who are yet to come have given up this body
And are subject to destruction. Therefore,
Abide in the doctrine and practise with determination.

The *Sutra of Advice for a King* says,

Suppose four great mountains in the four directions solid, stable, essential, uncrumbled, uncracked, unblemished, very hard, extremely dense, and touching the sky were to be overturned, the grass, forests, tree-trunks, branches, all the leaves, all the living beings and creatures would be crushed into the smallest particles. This would not easily be avoided by escaping quickly or with strength, nor by wealth, substances, mantras or medicine.

O great king, likewise the four great fears cannot easily be avoided by escaping quickly or with strength, nor by substances, mantra, or medicine. What are these four? old age, sickness, death, and decline. O great king, old age comes with the destruction of youth, sickness with the destruction of health, decline comes with the destruction of all your fortune, and death comes with the destruction of life. They cannot easily be avoided by escaping quickly or with strength, nor with wealth, substances, mantras, or medicine.

Secondly, reflect that as you cannot increase your lifespan, it constantly declines, so death is inevitable. Not only is your lifespan brief, but it decreases continually, as years are exhausted by the passing of months, months by the passing of days, and days by the passing of nights. As Shantideva says in *Guide to the Bodhisattva's Way of Life*,

Life is always slipping by
And can never be increased,
Why will death not come to one like me?

This should be contemplated by means of examples. *Special Verses Collected by Topic* says,

Just as weaving yarn
Stretched back and forth across a loom
Finally runs out,
So too does every person's life.

Just as every step of one condemned
Brings him ever closer
To the executioner,
So too is every person's life.

Just as the flow of a waterfall
Can never be reversed,
So a person's life runs on
Without increase and beyond recall.

Hard to find and yet so brief
And giving rise to so much pain,
Lives are quickly destroyed,
Like the writing of a stick on water.

Just as the shepherd with his staff
Drives his flock into the fold,
So old age and sickness
Deliver people to the Lord of Death.

The *Extensive Sport Sutra* says,

The three realms are as fleeting as autumn clouds,
The birth and death of beings unfolds like a play,
Their lives, rushing away like a mountain stream,
Vanish like a flash of lightning.

Thirdly, the way to think about the certainty of death and the rarity of being able to practise the doctrine in this life is as follows. The *Sutra on Entering into the Womb* says,

> Half our lives are spent asleep. Until we are ten we are children and after twenty we grow old. Then there are hundreds of other obstructions, misery, lamentation, suffering, depression, even quarrelling and various physical ailments which limit our opportunity to practise.

Geshey Che-ka-wa said,

> Out of sixty years, if you take away the time spent on livelihood and sickness, there is barely five years directed towards the doctrine.

Birth Stories says,

> Alas, the world is filled with disturbing emotions, an unreliable and unpleasant place to live. The glory of this water-lily will soon become but a memory, such is the fate of all beings. It is surprising that people still do not feel afraid even though all roads are blocked by the Lord of Death. They are thoughtlessly lost in enjoyment. The destructive enemies, disease, old age and death, are powerful and unavoidable. When they are certainly heading for danger in future lives, how can the wise enjoy any happiness?

The *Letter to King Kanika* says,

> The Lord of Death is merciless,
> He kills a skilful man for no purpose.
> When death is so fast approaching,
> What wise man can live at ease.

Eventually the invincible warrior
Will shoot his unbearable arrows,
Before the inevitable occurs
It is in our interest to be prepared.

THE UNCERTAINTY OF THE TIME OF DEATH

Contemplation of the uncertainty of the time of death is also divided into three. Firstly, consider that the lifespan of the people of this world is uncertain, whereas the lifespan of the beings of the northern world is definite.[22] In some other worlds too the lifespan is uncertain, but in most of them it is definite, yet that of the beings of this southern world is extremely uncertain. *Treasury of Knowledge* says,

Ultimately (the lifespan of) this (world) is uncertain (whether the average) is ten years or immeasurable.

Special Verses Collected by Topic says,

Of many people seen in the morning,
Some will not be seen in the afternoon.
And of the many seen in the afternoon,
Some will not be seen the next morning.

And,

Since many men and women
Have died in the prime of life,
What guarantee is there that this one
Will not die because he is young.

Some die in the womb
And some immediately they're born.
Some die when they can crawl
And some when they've started to walk.

Some die when they're old
Some are young and in the prime of life.

Everyone passes away by turn
Like the dropping of ripened fruit.

Secondly, consider how many factors lead to death, while the conditions for life are few. The *Precious Garland* says,

Living amidst the causes of death
Is like a lamp in the wind.

The *Friendly Letter* says,

As life is as susceptible to harm
As a bubble buffeted by the wind,
It is really amazing that we have the chance
To breathe in, breathe out and awaken from sleep.

The *Four Hundred Verses* says,

Individual elements are powerless,
But assembled are known as a collection.
Well-being is their (balanced) opposition.

The *Precious Garland* says,

Many conditions are conducive to death,
Few are supportive of life
And even they lead to death.
Therefore, practise the doctrine always.

Thirdly, consider the uncertainty of the time of death due to the extreme fragility of the body. The *Friendly Letter* says,

If the earth, Mt. Meru, the oceans and embodied beings
Will be burnt up in the blaze of seven suns
So not even dust will remain,
What need is there to speak of human fragility.

The *Letter to King Kanika* says,

> The Lord of Death is no one's friend
> And his attack is sudden.
> So, without putting it off until tomorrow,
> Begin to practise the holy doctrine now.
> It is not a good idea
> To put it off until another day,
> For the time will come when you no longer exist
> And that could be tomorrow.

ONLY THE DOCTRINE CAN HELP AT THE TIME OF DEATH

At the time of death our relatives, friends, body and possessions are of no help. The *Letter to King Kanika* says,

> As the ripened fruit of past actions
> You will be completely abandoned.
> In accordance with your new actions
> You will be seized by the Lord of Death.
> Nothing but your virtues and misdeeds will escort you.
> Since all will return to their destinies,
> No one will accompany you.
> Understanding this, please practise well.

Shrī Jagatamitra said (in his *Letter to Chandrarāja*),

> Even if you possess the wealth of a god,
> In the next world after your death
> You will be as one attacked in a barren land:
> Alone, deprived of princes and queens,
> With no clothes and bereft of friends,
> Dispossessed of kingdom and castle,
> Although you may have great power and strength.
> Nothing is to be seen and nothing heard,
> Not one single person can follow you.
> In short, when not even your name
> Will then exist, what else is there to say?

Contemplating in this way how ultimately death is certain, its time is uncertain, and at that time nothing is of any help except the doctrine, resolve to practise it now. Within the holy doctrine meditation on the awakening mind is the primary practice. Having ascertained this, everything will become a factor of the training in the awakening mind.

ACTIONS AND THEIR CONSEQUENCES

After death we do not cease to exist, but have to take rebirth. Our place of birth will be either happy or miserable according to our actions rather than our free will. Therefore, it is reasonable to try to cultivate good actions properly and avoid bad ones. This contemplation has four parts.

THE CERTAINTY OF ACTIONS AND THEIR RESULTS

All instances of happiness or suffering, whether coarse or subtle, are the result of specific wholesome and unwholesome actions. The *Precious Garland* says,

> All sufferings are the result of unwholesome actions,
> So, likewise are all bad rebirths.
> The pleasure enjoyed throughout our lives
> And all happy rebirths are the result of virtue.

THE MULTIPLYING NATURE OF ACTIONS

A small wholesome or unwholesome cause can give rise to a much greater happy or miserable result. *Special Verses Collected by Topic* says,

> Performing even the smallest misdeed
> Will lead to great fear
> And trouble in future lives,
> Like poison that has entered the body.

Creating even a small meritorious act
Will bring forth great joy in future lives
And fulfil the great purpose,
Like grain ripening into a bumper crop.

The same text further says,

Just as the shadow of the bird
Accompanies it in the sky,
So beings follow after
Wholesome and unwholesome actions.

Just as the traveller with few provisions
Will suffer on the road,
So, sentient beings who do not do good
Will come to a bad end.

Just as the traveller with plentiful provisions
Will have an enjoyable journey,
So, sentient beings who have done good
Will go to a happy rebirth,

And,

We should not do even the smallest wrong
Thinking it will do no harm,
For the accumulation of drops of water
Will gradually fill a large vessel,

And,

Don't think, 'The little wrongs I've done
Will make no difference later.'
For just as single water drops
Gradually fill a large vessel,
So ordinary beings become filled with wrongs
Collected little by little.

Don't think, 'The little virtues I've done
Will make no difference later.'
For just as single water drops

> Gradually fill a large vessel,
> So the steadfast are filled with virtue
> Collected little by little.

NOT HAVING TO FACE THE CONSEQUENCES OF ACTIONS YOU HAVE NOT DONE

If you have not accumulated an action, whether it would give rise to pleasure or pain, you will not experience its consequence. Those who enjoy the fruits of the infinite merits accumulated by the Teacher do not have to collect all their causes, but they must at least do their part.

ONCE COMMITTED ACTIONS DO NOT FADE AWAY

The *Especially Exalted Praise* says,

> The Brahmins say that virtues and misdeeds
> Can be given away and transferred,
> But you teach that actions done do not fade away
> And actions not done have no consequences

The *King of Meditative Stabilisations Sutra* also says

> It is impossible not to encounter the results of your deeds,
> But you won't feel the results of those done by others.

The *Transmission of Discipline* says,

> Even after hundreds of aeons actions are not exhausted
> If they meet with the assembled conditions
> Then embodied beings
> Will meet with their results.

So, remembering the certainty and multiplying nature of karma, that an action not done will yield no result, and that once done an action will not fade away, will obstruct all that gives rise to the path of black actions. You must earnestly engage in white, wholesome actions and since training in the precious awakening mind is considered to be the principal and supreme virtue, all of them should be part of that training.

THE DRAWBACKS OF CYCLIC EXISTENCE

THE DISADVANTAGES OF UNCERTAINTY

In cyclic existence relationships with friends and enemies are very changeable. Things of this world are not at all reliable, they are miserable. The *Friendly Letter* says,

> Your father becomes your son, your mother your wife,
> And your enemies become friends.
> The opposite also takes place. Therefore,
> In cyclic existence there is no certainty at all.

The *Questions of Subāhu Sutra* says,

> At times enemies turn out to be friends
> And similarly friends turn into foes.
> Likewise, anyone can become your father or mother,
> And even your parents can become your foes.
> Because friendship is changeable like this,
> The intelligent shun attachment.
> The misconceived thought that relations are pleasant
> Is replaced by the joy of engaging in virtue.

THE DISADVANTAGES OF DISSATISFACTION

The *Friendly Letter* says,

> Each individual has drunk more milk
> Than the four great oceans, yet

In the ordinary person's continuing cyclic existence
There is still more to be drunk,

the point can be taken from this. The same text says,

Understand attachment to objects of desire as being
Like a leper's seeking for comfort, when,
Tormented by maggots, he sits
By the fire, but finds no relief.

The *Condensed Perfection of Wisdom Sutra* says,

Obtaining everything you desire
And consuming much on a daily basis,
Yet still to be dissatisfied
Is the greatest disease.

So, there is no satisfaction in sensual pleasure and if you think especially about what is taught in the *Sutra on Avoiding Sorrow*, you will feel great concern. It says,

The water in the ocean
Bears no comparison
With the molten copper you've drunk
Again and again in hell.

The amount of filth you've eaten
When you were born as a pig or dog,
Would be much greater than
Meru, the king of mountains.

As a vessel for all the tears
You have shed, when parted
From friends and relatives in cyclic existence,
The ocean would not be big enough.

> If all the heads cut off
> In the course of mutual conflicts
> Were to be piled up, the heap
> Would reach beyond the realm of Brahma.
>
> Born many times as a famished worm,
> The amount of earth and dung you've eaten
> Would fill the great ocean of milk
> Right up to the brim.

So, as explained, however much worldly wealth you acquire, it is nothing but seduction. You should feel apprehensive, thinking of how the same could happen to you if you do not make further effort. In the words of the spiritual friend Sang-phu-wa,

> From the first you must face so many ups and downs here in cyclic existence, but nothing worthwhile. Think about this until you are convinced.

THE DISADVANTAGES OF HAVING TO DISCARD YOUR BODY OVER AND OVER AGAIN

The bodies assumed by each sentient being have to be discarded, if their bones did not rot, they would be greater than Mt. Meru. (The *Friendly Letter* says,)

> The heap of each sentient being's bones
> Would equal or even be greater than Mt. Meru.

THE DISADVANTAGES OF ENTERING THE WOMB OVER AND OVER AGAIN

(The same text says,)

> The earth would be insufficient to count the number of one's mothers
> With pellets of soil the size of juniper berries.

The commentary to the *Friendly Letter* quotes a sutra as follows,

> O Bhikṣhus, if a person were to take pellets of earth the size of juniper berries, saying, 'This is my mother, this is my mother's mother, and so forth,........' as he casts them aside, O Bhikṣhus, the soil of this great earth would soon be exhausted, but the series of that person's mothers would not.

THE DISADVANTAGES OF CONTINUALLY CHANGING FROM HIGH TO LOW

The *Friendly Letter* says,

> Having been Shakra,[23] worthy of the world's veneration,
> One falls again to earth through the force of action,
> Or having been a Universal Monarch,
> One again becomes a servant in cyclic existence.
>
> Having long experienced the pleasure of fondling
> The breasts and hips of celestial maidens,
> One undergoes the unbearable contact of the crushing,
> Cutting and slashing operations in the hells.
>
> Think of how, following the pleasure of the ground's
> Yielding at the touch of your feet, while dwelling
> Long on Meru's peak, the unbearable suffering of the
> Fire-pit and the Swamp of Filth will strike again.
>
> Having frolicked in lovely pleasant gardens
> Waited on by celestial maidens, again your
> Arms and legs, ears and nose are cut
> In the Forest of Trees with Leaves Like Swords.
>
> After resting in gently flowing streams
> On golden lotuses with beautiful celestial maidens,
> Again you fall into the unbearably caustic,
> Boiling water of the infernal Fordless River.

> Having attained the magnificent pleasure of celestial
> Realms, and even Brahma's bliss of detachment,
> Again you undergo endless suffering
>
> As kindling for the fires of the Hell Without Respite.
> When you have attained the state of sun or moon,
> The light of your body illuminates the entire world,
> But on returning to darkness again, not even
> Your outstretched hand can be seen.

The *Transmission of Discipline* says,

> The end of all accumulation is exhaustion,
> The end of being high is to fall low,
> The end of meeting is separation,
> The end of life is death.

THE DISADVANTAGES OF HAVING NO COMPANIONS

(The *Friendly Letter* says,)

> As the disadvantages are like this, take up
> The lamplight of the three kinds of merit,
> For you enter the infinite darkness,
> Where sun and moon cannot reach, alone.

These six disadvantages can be abbreviated in three points: cyclic existence is unreliable, whatever pleasures are enjoyed in cyclic existence are ultimately unsatisfying, and this has been so for beginningless time.

The first can be explained in four ways. Obtaining a body is not to be relied upon since it has to be discarded again and again. We cannot rely on receiving help or harm since nothing is certain. We cannot rely on finding prosperity because our position changes from high to low. The fellowship of others cannot be relied upon since we have to go unaccompanied.

(The second point concerns the evident disadvantages of dissatisfaction.)

The third point indicates that because we have entered the womb over and over again, the origin of our series of births is untraceable. Do the abbreviated contemplation in this way. To develop courage the *Friendly Letter* says,

> Become disgusted with cyclic existence,
> The source of so much suffering: not getting
> What you want, death, sickness, old age and so on.

Think about the eight kinds of suffering explained above. In this way, think about the three sufferings of cyclic existence in general and each of the six sufferings in particular. If you think about them from many angles you will come to see the disadvantages of cyclic existence from a broad perspective. If you think about them intensely, you will develop a strong understanding and if you think about them for a long time, you will develop a lasting understanding of the disadvantages of cyclic existence. When understanding the disadvantages of cyclic existence gives rise to a determination to be free, you should know that the precious awakening mind is the main, supreme path to liberation from cyclic existence and that this should form a part of the training in the awakening mind. This concludes the way to think about the preliminary teaching.

CULTIVATING THE CONVENTIONAL AWAKENING MIND

There are two approaches to the basic practice of developing the precious awakening mind: that dealing with the process of training in the conventional awakening mind and that involving the process of cultivating the ultimate awakening mind. The former includes an explanation of how we are able to enter the great vehicle only by activating the altruistic mind of enlightenment and is followed by a description of the actual techniques for cultivating the precious awakening mind. (The latter, dealing with the development of the view of emptiness, will be dealt with later.)

Appreciating the value of the awakening mind, the entrance to the great vehicle

Since it is necessary to embark upon the great vehicle, as pointed out above, you may wonder what is the entrance to such activity. In stating that there are two aspects to the great vehicle, the practices of the transcending perfections and those of secret mantra, Buddha, the Conqueror, has made it clear that there is no great vehicle practice other than these two. Furthermore, the entrance to each of them is only by means of the awakening mind. The moment it arises in your mental continuum, even if you have not generated any other quality, you become a follower of the great vehicle. On the contrary, the moment it is lost, you fall to the level of the (low vehicle) Hearers and so on, even though you may possess such qualities as an understanding of emptiness. Such a falling away from the great vehicle is referred to in many great vehicle scriptures and can also be established by reason.

So, whether you are considered a practitioner of the great

vehicle or not depends simply on whether you possess this attitude. In fact, the great vehicle is indicated by nothing but the presence or absence of this very state of mind. In this context the *Guide to the Bodhisattva's Way of Life* says,

> The instant the awakening mind is activated
> Those bound up in the prison of cyclic existence
> Come to be known as sons of the Buddhas Gone to Bliss,

And,

> Today I've been born into the family of the Buddhas
> And have become a son of the awakened ones.

This shows that as soon as you generate the awakening mind, you become a son or daughter of the Conquerors. The *Life-story of the Exalted Maitreya* also says,

> O child of my family, here are some analogies. (The awakening mind) is like a diamond, even a fragment of which surpasses all other kinds of valuable ornaments such as gold, which retains the name diamond and can eradicate all poverty. O child of my family, in the same way the precious diamond-like mind which gives rise to omniscience, even when it is weak, outshines all the golden qualities adorning the Hearers and Solitary Realisers. Because of it you retain the name Bodhisattva and eradicate all the poverty of cyclic existence.

So, even though your conduct may not be distinguished, if you have engendered such a mind, you are referred to as a Bodhisattva, an awakening warrior. The protector Nāgārjuna writes in his *Precious Garland*,

> If you and the world wish to attain
> Unsurpassable full awakening,
> The source is the awakening mind,
> Which should be as stable as the King of Mountains.

The *Vajrapāni Initiation Tantra* also says,

> 'O great Bodhisattva, the great mysteries of this extremely vast mandala of *dharani*[24], which are extremely profound, unfathomable, rare and secret, should not be revealed to evil beings. O Vajrapāni, what you have said is unique and extremely rare. Therefore, how is one to explain it to those beings who have never heard it before?'
>
> To this Vajrapāni replied, 'O Mañjushrī, at such a time that anyone, who is engaged in meditation on the awakening mind, has achieved that state of mind, then O Mañjushrī, those who perform the activities of a Bodhisattva, specifically the activities involving secret mantra, should enter into the dharani mandala by receiving the great wisdom initiation. Anyone who has not accomplished the awakening mind should not engage in these (practices). They should neither view nor enter the mandala. To them the gestures and details of secret mantra should never be shown.

This is also stated in the *Array of Tree Trunks Sutra*,

> O child of my family, the awakening mind is like the seed of all the teachings of the Buddhas. It is like the field in which the positive actions of all wandering beings prosper. It is like the earth on which the whole world depends. It is like the son of the Lord of Wealth who completely eliminates all kinds of poverty. It is like the father completely protecting all Bodhisattvas. It is like the king of wish-granting jewels which perfectly fulfils every purpose. It is like the miraculous vase which acts to accomplish every wish. It is like a spear vanquishing the foe of disturbing emotions. It is like armour guarding you from improper thoughts. It is like a sword beheading the disturbing emotions. It is like an axe felling the tree of disturbing emotions. It is like a weapon staving off all kinds of attack. It is like the hook which draws you out of the waters of

> cyclic existence. It is like the whirlwind which scatters all mental obstructions and their sources. It is like the condensed teaching that encompasses all the prayers and activities of the Bodhisattvas. It is like the shrine before which all the gods, humans and demigods of the world can present their offerings. O child of my family, the awakening mind is endowed like this with these and immeasurable other excellent qualities.

So, the awakening mind is explained in this way as the exclusive entrance for venturing into the great vehicle that enables you to accomplish the state of a completely awakened being. The moment it is born within your mindstream, all the obstructions from previously accumulated actions are burnt up. It acts to protect you from all miseries and fears. It begins to provide you with the inexhaustible fruits of higher states of rebirth and the definite goodness of liberation. It is like the quintessential butter arising from the churning of the ocean of scriptures. It is like the seed that is the exclusive proximate cause leading you to the fully awakened state of being.

In realising such benefits of the awakening mind, your heart-strings should resound with joy, for although life as a free and fortunate human being generally provides you with an opportunity to practise the sacred doctrine, the wonderful discovery of the chance to practise the awakening mind specific to the great vehicle is sure to be a source of great encouragement. This is an event of major importance.

ACTUAL TECHNIQUES FOR CULTIVATING THE AWAKENING MIND

The stages for training the mind are explained in two sections: the actual training in the conventional awakening mind and the five precepts that are factors of the training. The actual training deals with the conventional awakening mind concerned with the welfare of others, which is explained by means of the teaching on exchanging yourself with others and the ways to cultivate the awakening mind that is actually concerned with the interests of others, and the awakening mind concerned with attaining the fully awakened state of being.

EXCHANGING YOURSELF WITH OTHERS THROUGH ACKNOWLEDGING THE FAULTS OF SELFISHNESS AND THE ADVANTAGES OF CONCERN FOR OTHERS

The great pioneers[25] have explained that, in general, cultivating the awakening mind involves the twofold activity of being concerned with the welfare of others and being concerned with enlightenment. With regard to the first, we should see those sentient beings who are the object of our concern as being equally pleasing and agreeable. The ways to achieve this include being led through the method of seven causes and one result. Having realised that relatives arouse feelings of pleasure, enemies arouse feelings of unease and those who are neither give rise to feelings of indifference, meditate on all sentient beings as being close to you. Although in reality (all sentient beings) are not your mother, by meditating on recognising them as your mother, remembering their kindness, and wishing to repay it, generate a sense of their being attractive.

According to the training that follows the exalted Shānti-deva's tradition, once we have grasped the many disadvantages of a self-centred attitude we will be inclined to give it up and realising the many benefits of appreciating others, we will generate a sense of sentient beings, who are the object of our concern, as being attractive, pleasing and dear to us.

Since the great Conqueror's Son, Che-ka-wa's technique for cultivating the awakening mind relies upon the latter (of these two approaches), his explanation has two sections: showing what is to be given up by contemplating the disadvantages of selfishness and showing what is to be put into practice through contemplating the benefits of concern for others.

WHAT IS TO BE GIVEN UP BY CONTEMPLATING THE DISADVANTAGES OF SELFISHNESS

Banish the one to blame for everything

We sentient beings run after misery that we do not desire and never achieve what we wish. At the root of it all we seek to lay the blame elsewhere, which is a mistake. This is because all the various lengthy and violent sufferings that come from being born among the five or six kinds of existence, from the Hell Without Respite to the Peak of Existence, are not without causes, nor do they arise from unrelated causes. These come about in dependence upon the actions and disturbing emotions that give rise to everything. Since actions are caused by disturbing emotions, disturbing emotions are the primary factor. Moreover, amongst the disturbing emotions it is the ignorance that clutches onto a misconception of self[26] that is the principal source of all misery. The *Guide to the Bodhisattva's Way of Life* says,

However much torment, fear
And suffering there is in the world,
It all arises from the misconception of self.
O, what trouble this great ghost brings me?

Furthermore, since disturbing emotions, chiefly created by seizing onto a misconception of self, bring us harm, they are the actual adversary. We should not maintain relations with this long term antagonist. The same text says,

Thus, through long, unbroken contact he is our foe,
Sole cause of an ever increasing heap of trouble.
When we are certain of this in our hearts,
How can we be happy and unafraid in cyclic existence?

Moreover, we can attribute all these harms to our selfish attitude and, thinking of how it slams the door on all benefits and accomplishments, we should beware of it. Likewise, the self-centred attitude is an expression of stupid ignorance, since this lack of consideration for others is like taking hold of the sharp weapon of wrong views and slaughtering any concern for good and bad deeds. So, right here within us is an evil butcher who cuts off the source of a life of high status and definite goodness. This selfish thought, holding up the bag of the three poisons, is the thief within us, who destroys our harvest of virtue. By collecting rotten worthless things in the cave of our heart, we have here within us an owl-headed deceiver who attracts all human and inhuman interferences.

In the fields of action are planted the seeds of consciousness. Irrigating them over and over again with the waters of desire and craving is the farmer here within us who cultivates the numerous shoots of the five or six kinds of suffering beings. Even though the previous Buddhas, the Transcendent Subduers have spent as long as us in this beginningless world, we have been unable to adhere to any of the excellent qualities of this or the world beyond. So, here within us is a naked, empty-handed slob behaving over-indulgently.

Wherever we are born, from the Peak of Existence to the Hell Without Respite, we dwell in misery. Whoever we befriend is a friend of suffering. Whatever objects we use are nothing but objects of anguish. These are the words of the Buddha, the Transcendent Subduer, found in the texts of the learned masters who commented on his thought and are to be heard in the songs of realisation of the supreme spiritual masters. Yet, even though this is definitely the case, like an old dog attracted to a scrap of food, the glutton within us is constantly engrossed in the marvels of cyclic existence.

When a mediator intervenes to pacify military conflicts, much confusion arises from a fundamental uncertainty over whether benefit will or will not be forthcoming. So it is with us, because of a fundamental uncertainty about whether our fears will lead to trouble or not, we have within us a coward who can only guess whether the barrier he constructs will suffice to allay his fears that one major hurt will ruin him again.

We fight with swords, arrows and spears in hope of gaining victory and profit, and when we lose we console ourselves by accusing somebody else. We have within us an evil being who shamelessly blames all problems on our learned teachers and abbots, our friends, and those dear to us, our parents and relatives.

We are jealous of everyone, from the highest spiritual friend to the lowliest louse. We are competitive with equals, arrogant towards inferiors, become conceited when praised and angry when criticised or abused. Like the roaming of an unbridled horse, of all the disturbing emotions within us, this is the most restless.

We should never fool ourselves about the fact that happiness arises from virtue and suffering arises from evil. This is assured, has been stated by the Transcendent Subduer, is written in texts by learned masters elaborating his thought, and can be heard in the glorious, holy masters' songs of spiritual realisation. Everyone desires happiness and wishes for not even the slightest misery, yet when others encourage us in the direction of wholesome conduct, we fail to heed their words. We engage in proscribed and natural misdeeds like water pouring downhill and act reluctantly to restrain them. Here within us is an evil holder of wrong views, whose promises are completely contradicted by the way he behaves.

For a beginningless time we have been circling through cyclic existence because of the eighty-four thousand disturbing emotions. This also applies to the numerous troubles and pains we have experienced until today. Yet, despite having closed many doors to the achievement of benefit and pleasure, we still lack the vision to see even the slightest defect in any of this. Here within us is a clay image with blind eyes.

In brief, if our actions of body, speech and mind are done under the influence of a self-centred attitude, the source of all misery and conflict, they will bring upon us all the trouble of external foes and internal disturbances. Holding ourselves dear is like the blue-headed bird of ill-omen. Therefore, now that we understand that we are to give up neglecting others, we should hold selfishness as our principal enemy and set it apart as a foe. As the exalted Shāntideva has said,

> Those earlier times when you overcame me are past
> Now I see you in another (light)
> And wherever you go
> I shall destroy your arrogance.
>
> Having sold you to others, I shall not be upset
> At having offered you into their service.
> If I should be negligent
> And not give you to other sentient beings,
>
> You will certainly deliver me
> To the guardians of hell.
> If that should take place,
> My misery will be interminable.
>
> Now, recalling my grudges against you
> I shall destroy your concern for your own good.

We should keep this in mind.

Besides, due to the strength of our acquaintance with a self-centred attitude over beginningless time, if we hear the squealing of rats in a house, we are frightened of them nibbling our nose. Hearing a clap of thunder we worry that our heads will be struck by lightning, and coming to a haunted place we are afraid. It is you (the self-centred attitude) that causes our fear. Similarly, there are some who suffer from fear of bad talk, and some who are upset at being unable to restrain their enemies and others who are distressed at being unable to support their family and friends. In short, in whatever ways and by whatever means they are tormented, we should realise that selfishness is the source of blame.

Geshey Na-mo-wa has suggested, 'While you are chopping your brick tea[27], saying "come on, down with you," think that you are pounding on the head of your own selfishness.'

Geshey Ben has also advised, 'I will stand guard at the doorway of my mind with the sharp spear of mindfulness. If he attacks, I will attack. If he relents, I will relent.'

Also Lang-ri-t'ang-pa has said, '"Give profit and victory to sentient beings." Why? Because the accumulation of all kinds of goodness arises in reliance upon them. "Take loss and defeat upon yourself." Why? Because all harm and suffering comes from holding yourself dear.'

If we practise in this way, then just as a person can be laid low by food poisoning, so our self-centred attitude will be defeated. So long as we cannot do this, even if we load a yak with monastic robes, or have the empowering vase placed on our heads a thousand times, or listen to the doctrine for our entire lives, or give up everything mundane, no matter how we try we will not achieve the object of our desire. We will be restless with pain, like the mongoose in grief over the death of its offspring. Instead we will have to draw in our thumbs without extending them to others, begging for help. If we can persevere as advised, it is taught that we will become followers of the great vehicle, our minds will become expansive, we will be able to elevate others and we will develop great wisdom.

Essentially, if all the Buddhas of the three times were to teach for aeons about the disadvantages of the disturbing emotions that arise out of a self-centred attitude, they would never end. However, the above explanation, contained in the Buddha's teachings, the commentaries to them and the instructions of the supreme spiritual masters, is a means for making us aware of the defects of our own attitude. Think about it again and again, test it and become convinced of it.

If we do this, whatever our external behaviour may be, our mindstreams will be mixed with the doctrine and our aims will be fulfilled. But, if we do not, all those things labelled as qualities will only serve to gratify our self-centred attitude. Within us will be the friendly relative who provokes and increases our disturbing emotions.

WHAT IS TO BE PUT INTO PRACTICE THROUGH CONTEMPLATING THE ADVANTAGES OF CONCERN FOR OTHERS

Meditate on the great kindness of all beings

Chandrakīrtī states in his *Supplement to (Nāgārjuna's) 'Treatise on the Middle Way'* that in general, for a person to belong to the lineage of the great vehicle, love and compassion are vitally important at the beginning, middle and end of his or her practice. Both are developed in dependence on sentient beings: love, by focusing on the fact that sentient beings are bereft of happiness, and sympathetic great compassion by focusing on the fact that sentient beings are afflicted by suffering like a raging bonfire. The *Guide to the Bodhisattva's Way of Life* says,

> That we make offerings to whoever has a mind of love
> Also reflects the value of sentient beings.

In addition, the awakening mind that seeks to gain unsurpassable enlightenment must be preceded by love and compassion, which in turn are developed in dependence on sentient beings. Seeing that only a fully awakened being has the ability to eliminate every last hindrance and misery and establish every single sentient being without exception in a state of happiness and well-being, stirred by love and compassion we should activate the awakening mind that wishes to attain that completely awakened state of being. (Maitreya/Asaṅga's *Ornament for Clear Realisation* says,)

> Generating the (awakening) mind is the desire for
> Completely perfected full awakening for others' sake.

The four ways of amassing disciples (giving, speaking pleasantly, teaching and acting in accordance with the teachings) and the six transcending perfections (generosity, ethics, patience, enthusiasm, meditative stability and discriminating intelligence) are also developed in dependence on sentient beings, as is abiding in and repeatedly enhancing the awakening mind.

Therefore, we can see that the basis of our conduct, the source of the awakening mind, love and compassion, the basis of the practice, the generation of the (altruistic) mind and the essence of our own training arise in dependence on sentient beings. The accumulation of all manner of causes for accomplishing the fruit of buddhahood depends upon sentient beings. Even after the highest attainment of complete awakening, the practice of enlightened activity, which comes about in an unbroken stream, arises in dependence upon the sentient beings for whom it is done. Essentially, at the root of everything in the great vehicle, the causes and the result, is concern for sentient beings. (As the *Guide to the Bodhisattva's Way of Life* says,)

> Whenever I turn my gaze upon a sentient being
> Thinking, 'I shall fully awaken
> Through depending upon this being,'
> I should look at her with open-hearted love.

Moreover, if, for instance, we plant healthy seeds in an extremely fertile field, guarding them well against marauders, we will reap a bountiful harvest. Understanding this we will treat our fine field with great care. Likewise, having planted the potent seeds of love, compassion, the awakening mind, the six transcending perfections and the four means of amassing disciples in the field of sentient beings, if we look after them well, they will give rise to the state of a fully awakened being, a Transcendent Subduer, fulfilling the two purposes (of ourselves and others). Understanding this we will take great care of the field of sentient beings and, seeing them as pleasing and attractive, we will respect them. The *Guide to the Bodhisattva's Way of Life* says,

> Therefore the Mighty One has stated that there are
> The field of sentient beings and the field of Buddhas,

For many who have pleased them
Have thereby reached perfection.

Since the qualities of full awakening are derived
From sentient beings and Conquerors alike,
How can we act respectfully towards Conquerors
And not towards sentient beings?
We should not foster such an attitude.

In addition, seeing sentient beings as the source of the cause and result of full awakening, they are all worthy of our highest respect. The same text says,

Even if, in order to pay respect to someone
In whom a mere portion of good qualities
Of the unique collection of excellence exists, we were
To present the three realms, it would be insufficient.

Since all sentient beings have
A portion of Buddha's supreme qualities,
For this reason alone
Sentient beings are worthy of respect.

It is said that accomplishing the welfare and happiness of sentient beings, gives rise to higher status and definite goodness. Whereas, every kind of trouble arises from neglecting sentient beings. In his *Commentary on the Awakening Mind* Nāgārjuna states,

In this world, pleasant and miserable existences
Are the desired and unwanted results
That arise (respectively) from
Helping or harming sentient beings.
Should you rely on sentient beings,
You will gain the unsurpassable fully awakened state,
There is not a single person in the three realms
Who has not taken birth as Brahma, Indra,

Or Vishnu, the protectors of the world,
Solely through helping sentient beings.
What could be more marvellous than that?
The many types of suffering
Experienced by sentient beings
As hell denizens, animals and hungry spirits,
Arise from harming sentient beings.
The miseries of hunger and thirst, eating one another
And being overwhelmed by pains
That are unrelenting and difficult to avoid
Are the result of harming sentient beings.

A person of the low vehicle does not attain even a part of full awakening, because he neglects sentient beings, whereas a follower of the great vehicle, since he is deeply concerned for others, actualises unsurpassable buddhahood. The same text says,

You should vigorously reject as if it were poison
A lack of affection for sentient beings.
Since Hearers lack such a feeling,
Won't they attain an inferior enlightenment?
As those who never completely forsake sentient beings,
Will attain the enlightenment of complete awakening,
How could those who examine the results
Of harming or helping others
Remain attached for a single instant
To their own welfare?

The harm sentient beings presently appear to be doing us is fundamentally caused by the disturbing emotions in our own mindstreams over beginningless time. The auxiliary conditions are the (tendencies remaining from) actual harm we have done against sentient beings over beginningless time. Due to the activation of such causes and conditions, those who harm us are motivated by evil thoughts, for which reason they engage in numerous cruel and misguided acts against us. In general, throughout limitless cyclic existence the blame for our experience of various miseries, such as those of the three bad rebirths in particular, rests with our self-centred attitude. As the exalted Shāntideva has said,

> Having been provoked by my actions,
> Harm befalls me. If by their involvement
> Sentient beings are thrown into hell,
> Am I not destroying them?

Now especially, when we are entering the door of the great vehicle teachings, these beings harm us in many ways. Because they thereby create obstacles for themselves to enter the great vehicle doctrine, they will experience the sufferings of cyclic existence in general and the three bad rebirths in particular. We should feel compassion for their becoming vessels of the manifold sufferings of the bad rebirths.

Moreover, those who are harming us have in fact been our mothers countless times before. We have eaten their flesh, drunk their blood, gnawed their bones and worn their skins times beyond number. If all the milk and curd we have drunk were gathered together, a vessel the size of the three worlds would not contain it. The times we have killed, beaten and robbed them also cannot be counted. We have taken their kindness for granted on all those occasions and now should repay our debt to them, thinking, 'Remembering your kindness, this is my duty.'

Singling out those we apprehend (as enemies), we should enhance love and compassion by means of both giving (happiness) and taking on (suffering). We should particularly rely on those who harm us, since they provide the basis for us to practise patience. Even the six perfections arise from relying on them. Because these foes are an object of forbearance, we can meditate on patience. If we have patience, the two perfections (of generosity and ethics) will have preceded it and the other three (effort, meditative stability, and discriminating intelligence) will be derived from relying on it.

When we let our thoughts turn over the significance of this, we will realise that objectively it is our foes who place enlightenment in the palms of our hands. The great Che-ka-wa expressed it like this,

> Whether they are our enemies or dear ones,
> All are the objects of disturbing emotions.
> Seeing everyone as a spiritual friend
> Will bring happiness, even when you are alone.

We should practise just as he has advised.

For instance, a spiritual preceptor is extremely kind because he bestows the vows that are the cause for us to attain liberation and omniscience. Our enemy too is like that, because by relying on him we can perfect patience, which is a cause of great enlightenment. This is like the saying, 'Don't spit out delicious food once it is in your mouth.' The *Guide to the Bodhisattva's Way of Life* says,

> Therefore, like finding treasure in
> My house without any effort on my part,
> I should be delighted that my enemy
> Becomes my friend in my efforts for enlightenment.

And,

> When anyone abuses me, or even
> When others do me harm,
> When they afflict me in such ways as these
> May they all have the fortune to gain enlightenment.

The great Che-ka-wa has also said,

> Even when hurt is offered in return for help
> Respond by meditating on great compassion.
> In this world the superior man will accept
> Such misfortune, while leading others to goodness.

If we understand how to train our minds in this way, then,

just as we could wander across a plain of swords if we had physical courage, or journeying to the mythical jewel-islands we would need to seek no stones to throw at the vicious dogs, so a period will come when there is no time when we do not train the mind. This is the single meeting point of all teachings. If you have that it is like the saying, 'One doctrine for one man and that one teaching is purposeful.' Thus, since it has one purpose, you can call the doctrine the practice of the awakening mind or whatever name you like, as the saying goes about Pel-den Lha-mo,

> O hundred named lady with a thousand characteristics,
> By whatever name we invoke you, that is your name,
> However we imagine you, those are your qualities.

Lang-ri-tang-pa said,

> Recognise sentient beings as the mothers who give birth to the Conquerors of the three times........

He also said,

> The awakening mind is generated in dependence on sentient beings. But like the saying, 'whatever you do when wearing an iron helmet is unpleasant,' to entertain such thoughts that wherever you are you feel vexed when encountering other beings who displease you, is like being unhappy with the causes of enlightenment.

The exalted Shāntideva has concisely stated the advantages of being concerned about others and the faults of selfishness,

> What need is there to say more?
> The childish work for their own benefit,
> The Buddhas work for the welfare of others,
> Just look at the difference between them.

Thinking about this deeply we should see that all faults arise from selfishness, whereas all good qualities come from benevolence towards others. This means that we should be concerned about sentient beings, should be fond of them and think of them with affection. Therefore, we should keep up our efforts until our thoughts of concern for ourselves and neglect of others have changed places.

This concludes my brief account of how to exchange self and others.

ACTUALLY CULTIVATING THE AWAKENING MIND CONCERNED WITH THE INTERESTS OF OTHERS

This has two sections, taking the practice to heart in the context of an actual meditation session, and what to do after the meditation session. The first involves meditation on love and then on compassion.

MEDITATION ON LOVE

Practise a combination of giving and taking

When we meditate on love by such means as giving away our bodies, possessions and merit to others, we should firstly understand the benefits to be gained through so doing. Then we will be filled with a great eagerness to practise the actual techniques for activating love. The *King of Meditative Stabilisations Sutra* says,

> Were we to make as many infinitely huge offerings
> As the millions and billions of realms in the universe
> And were to offer them forever to the supreme beings
> It would not compare with a fraction of the mind of love.

So, the Buddha has said that the merit created through love is far greater than that derived from constantly offering objects of great value to Buddha-fields across the far reaches of the universe.

In the *Sutra on the Adornment of Mañjushrī's Realm* it is said,

> In the north-eastern direction, which is said to be adorned by one thousand realms of the universe of the extremely powerful awakened being Maheshvara, every sentient being experiences happiness like the bliss of those Bhikṣhus who are absorbed in meditation on the cessation (of suffering). Such good conduct extends over thousands of millions of years. Yet were one person in our world to generate love for all sentient beings for even as long as it takes to snap his fingers, the merit he produced would be far greater. So what need is there to mention the value of abiding day and night in (meditation on) love?

The *Precious Garland* says,

> Even giving three hundred delicacies
> Three times every day (to monks)
> Would not equal a part of the merit
> Of even one moment of love.
>
> You will be loved by gods and men
> And they will also offer you protection.
> You will experience mental ecstasy and much happiness
> And poison and weapons will do you no harm.
>
> You will effortlessly achieve your purpose
> And could be born in Brahma's realm.
> Even if you have not attained liberation,
> Through love the eight spiritual qualities are gained.

If you have love, gods and men will gather together under its force. Even the Conqueror, Buddha, defeated the malevolent forces of Mara through the power of love, therefore it is the supreme protection and so forth.

You might wonder about the source of the explanation for meditation on love through giving away your body, wealth and virtue. It is to be found in Shāntideva's *Guide to the Bodhisattva's Way of Life*, in the chapter concerning acceptance of the awakening mind in a formal ceremony. When the ceremony of actual acceptance is over, just before the actual pledges are recited, as the preceptor is describing the visualisation of love and compassion, you should give away your body, possessions and sources of virtue.

HOW TO DISPENSE YOUR BODY, POSSESSIONS AND VIRTUES IN GENERAL

Now follows a general explanation, according to the scriptures, of just how we give away (body, possessions and virtues). The purpose of giving them away is that in so doing we will complete the two collections of merit and wisdom, and this is the reason we should give them away. The *Guide to the Bodhisattva's Way of Life* says,

> I will give away without restriction
> My body, possessions and the virtue
> I have produced in the three times
> To accomplish the welfare of all beings.

From amongst these it is generally inappropriate to give away the body because it consists of unclean substances such as flesh and blood. For those who are eager, the way to do this is explained below. If the body is to be given away, the *Array of Tree Trunks Sutra* says,

> You should transform yourself into a wish-fulfilling body that sustains all wandering beings.

And the *Sutra of the Vajra Victory Banner* says,

> Just as through various means and through various manifestations, the four great elements sustain all sentient beings, a Bodhisattva transforms his own body so that it is the basis for sustaining all sentient beings.

And the *Guide to the Bodhisattva's Way of Life* says,

> During the intermediate aeon of famine
> May I become food and drink
> For sentient beings who are poor and famished;
> May I remain in their presence as various necessities.

And,

> May I protect those without protection
> And be a guide leading those upon the path.
> May I become a vessel, a bridge and a ship
> For those who wish to cross over (the ocean).
>
> May I be an island for those searching for land
> And a lamp for those needing a light.
> May I become a bed for those who need rest
> And a servant for all who want assistance.
>
> May I become accomplishing mantras and excellent vases
> Fabulous wish-fulfilling trees and
> Great elements such as the earth.
> May I be the basis of sustenance
> For limitless sentient beings,
> Existing eternally for them like space.
>
> In this way, just as all realms of sentient beings
> Are infinite like the expanse of the sky,
> May I become the basis for their sustenance
> Until they all attain the state beyond sorrow.

In the *Spiritual Levels of the Bodhisattva* Asaṅga says,

> Bodhisattvas who have gone into solitude and have

> gathered their thoughts inwardly, should purify their thoughts (of selfishness) and from the bottom of their hearts with sincere faith should practise generosity out of their concern for all, imagining a limitless, huge and expansive variety of things, as well as providing sentient beings with (actual) gifts. In so doing, a Bodhisattva will expand his accumulations of merit limitlessly and with little hardship. This is a practice for Bodhisattvas who are endowed with great intelligence.

What Asaṅga is teaching here can be explained in terms of giving to the inhabitants (who are living beings), and giving to the environment (which beings inhabit). The first of these involves giving to those not engaged in the spiritual path and offering to those who are.

GIVING TO THOSE NOT ENGAGED IN THE SPIRITUAL PATH

We should first give our bodies to the beings in the eight hot hells[28] such as the reviving hell. Then to the beings in the eight cold hells[29], such as the blistering hell. Then we should give to beings in the surrounding hells[30] and to beings in the occasional hells (where sufferings are felt intermittently). To these beings we should give whatever we can, transforming everything just as an alchemical elixir changes iron into gold.

We should imagine that (those beings) attain lives with the freedom and opportunity to practise the doctrine. We should think that they are enriched with the seven jewels of an exalted being[31], as well as the seven good qualities of high status[32].

Just as a precious wish-fulfilling jewel provides whatever we desire, such as food and clothing, so should we imagine that in giving away our bodies they grant all wishes, manifest as food imbued with one hundred flavours, clothing to the value of a thousand gold coins, mansions with five hundred floors, and excellent companions who act only as an inspiration, who are associated with enjoyment, who delight in whatever objects are to be enjoyed, and who, surrounded by their possessions, are replete with everything. They are also to be imagined as being favourable factors for the accomplishment of the very highest teachings of the great vehicle.

Similarly, since the principal external influence is a well-qualified and virtuous spiritual friend of the great vehicle, we should visualise our bodies as providing the bases for hearing, contemplating and practising the doctrine: external factors such as scriptures of sutra and tantra, and internal ones such as the seven jewels of an exalted being and the three precious trainings in ethics, meditative stability, and discriminating intelligence. Essentially, these generate love and compassion in individuals' mindstreams, acting as a wellspring for the awakening mind. We should then imagine that through their practice of the six transcending perfections they reach the culmination of the two accumulations, Buddhahood, where their mindstreams are endowed with the eternal delight of the perfect body of truth.[33]

Then, in the same way, think as before that sentient beings, including the thirty-six types of hungry spirits residing throughout the ten directions, also attain the immaculate delight of the perfect body of truth, by virtue of our having given away our bodies.

Next, we should repeat the meditation with respect to animals, whether they dwell in the oceans or are scattered across the land throughout all the realms of the universe.

Then, we should think likewise of giving our bodies to all human beings in realms throughout the ten directions of the universe: those living on the four main and the eight sub-continents[34], those born with freedom of movement and those without such freedom, as well as those who lack the opportunity to accomplish the path of liberation in their present lifetime. Then, in giving our bodies to those people who do not have the opportunity to achieve the path of liberation in this lifetime, we should imagine that, through their fulfilling all the external and internal factors for accomplishing the path of liberation, they gain (the same result as described) above.

Similarly, we should also give our bodies in their entirety to each sentient being abiding among the six kinds of gods of the desire realm[35], such as the four great kings, the twelve kinds of gods of the form realm, from those of the Brahma Family to those of the Great Result, as well as those of the four states of the formless realm who have not entered the path of liberation. We should imagine that these gods achieve the same goal as described before. We should also imagine giving in a like manner to beings in the intermediate state between death and rebirth.

GIVING IN PARTICULAR TO THOSE WHO HARM US

Having imagined creating various external necessities, such as food, clothing, and shelter, from our bodies, we invoke all harmful elements with the hook of the awakening mind. Then sincerely give them whatever they require. Generate a deep sense of closeness to them, thinking, 'You have all been my own mother on countless occasions over beginningless time. You have tried your utmost to help me in every possible way, saving me from misery and disaster.' Remember that in addition we owe them an immense debt, having eaten their flesh, gnawed their bones, drunk their blood and worn their skins. We have robbed them of their possessions, tortured them physically and taken their lives. We should recognise that we now have a responsibility to repay this debt of kindness.

Since this is their right, imagine their obtaining what they each wish in their respective forms, food for the hungry, clothes for the needy, shelter for the homeless, friends and servants for those who yearn for them. Of the foods, supply the three dairy products[36], the three sweets[37] and flesh and blood for those who want them. Give liberally without restraint. Let those who want flesh eat it, let those who want blood drink it, let those who want bones gnaw them, let those who want skins wear them. Whether they want raw food immediately or cooked food eventually, let them have it.

The moment we give to them, they eat, their bellies fill

and being relieved of hunger, thirst and poverty, they gain mental satisfaction. Their malicious thoughts and evil deeds are pacified. The altruistic intent of the awakening mind is born in their mindstreams, and the two collections are perfected. Imagine that thereby their mindstreams are imbued with the bliss of the perfect body of truth. There is a verse which says,

> The result of help is happiness
> And the fruit of harm is misery.
> See your own condition as an example
> And do not inflict harm on others.

The same practice of giving should be repeated towards all beings in every direction. Think of giving your body just as before to every sentient being without exception living in worlds in the eastern direction as numerous as grains of sand in the Ganges river. Then give likewise to those in the (other) main and sub-directions.

OFFERING TO THOSE WHO ARE ENGAGED IN THE SPIRITUAL PATH

Make offerings to the practitioners of the low vehicle by transforming your body into wish-fulfilling forms which meet their needs. Imagine that each one provides the practitioner with perfection of the two collections, the complete causes and conditions, inner and outer, to actualise the state of Buddha, the Transcendent Subduer, in this very life and that thereby they experience the bliss of the perfect body of truth in their mindstreams. In like manner offer your body to followers of the great vehicle, from those on the paths of accumulation and application up to the great Bodhisattvas on the tenth spiritual level. Think that they too obtain the bliss of the perfect body of truth in their mindstreams through the perfection of the two collections.

Next, offer your body to your direct spiritual masters, those belonging to their lineage and to the fully awakened beings residing in the infinite extensive worlds of the ten directions. Imagine creating many bodies before each of them and that these bodies have numerous arms and hands enabling us to offer innumerable prostrations, stimulated by an understanding of the advantages to be gained thereby, due to the process of actions and results. Furthermore, imagine immense heaps of inconceivable offerings emanated from this wish-granting body, and that thereby a great uncontaminated peace is born in their mindstreams. The *Guide to the Bodhisattva's Way of Life* says,

> May sentient beings repeatedly
> Make offerings to all the Buddhas,
> And may they constantly possess
> The inconceivable bliss of the Buddhas.
>
> May Bodhisattvas fulfil the welfare
> Of sentient beings as they wish to do
> And may all living beings receive
> All that the Buddhas have intended for them.
>
> Similarly, may the Solitary Buddhas
> And the Hearers enjoy peace.

This concludes the procedure for giving to the beings dwelling in the world.

GIVING TO THE ENVIRONMENT (WHICH BEINGS INHABIT)

To offer our bodies to the environment beings live in, we send them forth to infinite worlds within the ten directions in the aspect of wish-fulfilling jewels. Transform all impure environments filled with decayed logs, thorns, bushes, sand, crevices, cliffs and so forth, into wonderful pure lands in the nature of various precious stones, as level as the palm of your hand, open, extensive and smooth to touch, stainless and bright, perfumed with sandalwood, scattered with celestial flowers and fenced with jewels. They are filled with powdered gold, silver and pearls, and covered with utpala, lily and lotus flowers. There are beautiful lakes, pools and ponds containing water possessing the eight pleasing qualities, over which fly different kinds of water birds singing sweetly, enhancing the scene. Think that these constitute magnificent clouds of offerings to assemblies of Buddhas and exalted Bodhisattvas and that they do not for a moment provide the slightest cause for pride, arrogance or conceit in the beings who inhabit and enjoy the pleasures of these abodes. Think that on the contrary they realise enlightenment due to such favourable conditions. The *Guide to the Bodhisattva's Way of Life* says,

> May everywhere the earth be pure,
> Free from stones and pebbles,
> Level as the palm of my hand
> And smooth in the nature of aquamarine.
>
> May all embodied beings
> Uninterruptedly hear
> The sound of the doctrine issuing from birds
> Trees, beams of light and even from space.

GIVING AWAY POSSESSIONS

Those to whom we should give are in the same order as before. We should send forth our possessions, such as food, clothing, dwellings, companions, servants and so forth, in forms that fulfil all wishes. Imagine that extensively satisfying the needs of beings in all the worlds generates mundane and transcendental wealth, which creates the causes for accomplishing the fully awakened state and, after attaining enlightenment, their minds obtain the bliss of the perfect body of truth. As before, we subsequently offer wish-fulfilling wealth to the spiritual masters and Buddhas imagining that a special uncontaminated bliss is born in their mindstreams.

Giving away virtues

With regard to our bodies and possessions, we can give away what we have and what we will acquire in the future, but not that which has already ceased to exist. However, the virtues of the past, present and future are all suitable to be given away. The seeds or potencies of past virtues, as well as those of the present and all future virtues up to the attainment of Buddhahood can all be given away. The *Guide to the Bodhisattva's Way of Life* says,

> All virtues produced in the three times
> Should be given away without restraint
> To accomplish the goal of all sentient beings.

The master Nāgārjuna also says,

> By this virtue may all beings
> Gather the collections of merit and wisdom
> And as a result of that merit and wisdom
> May they achieve the two sublime bodies.

The *Questions of Gaganagañja Sutra* says,

> May whatever sources of virtue I have be transformed into sustenance for all sentient beings.

All these are ways of giving away virtues, from such weak virtues as the gift of a handful of food to an animal and incidental good deeds, to such powerful virtues as cultivation of the awakening mind. All of them should be dispensed to beings in all the worlds, as described above. Think that they each acquire the complete causes and conditions for attaining enlightenment and with the perfection of the two collections (of merit and wisdom) they awaken to enlightenment, possessing in their mindstreams the bliss of the perfect body of truth.

Should you wonder what is the use of training in the

thought of giving, it is that unless you train from now on, later you will be unable to make even the smallest gift, which will be an impediment. The *Questions of Subāhu Sutra* says,

> If you train the mind to give right away, with prolonged familiarity you will find no difficulty in actually giving away your body and so forth.

The *King of Meditative Stabilisations Sutra* also says,

> Just as the more you analyse something
> Your conceptions about it increase,
> So does your mind become acquainted with it.

Aryavīra said,

> However weak is your intention to benefit others
> You should always abide by this thought.
>
> Whoever has such a thought
> Will bring it to fulfilment.

The great Che-ka-wa said,

> The more you are acquainted with it,
> The more you purify conceptions.
> Take the help of many examples such as 'the seven generations.'[38]

In *Birth Stories* we read,

> May all my actions such as seeing, hearing, remembering, touching, or even conversing be of benefit to beings and may I always work to give them peace.

In this way, by practising generosity sincerely towards all sentient beings, we can instantly accumulate merits as innumerable as the beings themselves. The *Precious Garland* says,

> If the merits of speaking thus
> Could be given physical form,
> It would completely fill the whole of space
> And even overflow that.
>
> This was stated by the Subduer, Buddha,
> And supported by sound reasons,
> For just as the number of beings is beyond limit
> So is the intention to benefit them.

When we use the food, clothes and so on that we have sincerely dedicated to other beings, if we forget the welfare of others and use them with attachment to ourselves it is a deluded downfall. If it is done free from such attachment, but forgetful of others' interests, it is an undeluded downfall. If you have dedicated a certain thing to someone else, who knows it and has taken possession of that thing, and then, motivated by self-interest and an intention to steal, you make use of that thing, this qualifies as stealing and is a breach of the vows of individual emancipation, as the *Compendium of Training* makes clear. We should examine how a Bodhisattva should behave when he makes use of such things. If we make use of something with the intention of working for sentient beings there will be no moral fault. The *Compendium of Training* says,

> There will be no fault if you think, 'I shall use these with the intention of protecting both the possessions and their owner.'

This is similar to the case of a slave, who, always in the service of his master, has no belongings of his own. You might think that it is futile to dedicate your possessions to others since you are using them yourself. This is not so, the above text says,

Some, who have not realised suchness, lose faith in Bodhisattvas who practise in this way. This is unreasonable because such Bodhisattvas have a thorough realisation of the munificent thought of giving. It is therefore inappropriate for others to have doubts about how they behave.

MEDITATION ON COMPASSION

Now I shall explain the benefits of meditation on great compassion, repeated contemplation of which will increase your delight in it. The *Supplement to (Nāgārjuna's) 'Treatise on the Middle Way'* says,

> Because this alone is the excellent crop of the Conquerors,
> The propagated seed and the water that sustains it,
> And the fully ripened fruit at the time of harvest,
> I first pay tribute to great compassion.

With regard to its practical value the *Compendium of Perfect Doctrine* says,

> O Subduer, Bodhisattvas do not train in many teachings. O Subduer, if they perfectly grasp and accomplish one doctrine, they have enlightenment in the palms of their hands. If you ask, 'What is that doctrine?' it is great compassion. O Subduer, if you have great compassion, you have all doctrines in the palm of your hand. O Subduer, it is similar, for example, to the precious wheel of a universal monarch around which all other forces gather. O Subduer, similarly, wherever the great compassion of a Bodhisattva exists, there also exists the Buddha's doctrine. O Subduer, likewise, wherever the life faculty is present, there also are the sense faculties. O Subduer, thus, if you have great compassion, you will acquire all the other qualities of a Bodhisattva.

Compassion meditation has two parts: taking (sufferings) from the inhabitants, (living beings) and, taking (unsatisfactoriness) from the environment (which beings inhabit).

TAKING (SUFFERINGS) FROM INHABITANTS, (LIVING BEINGS)

The text says,

> *Giving and taking should be practised alternately*
> *And you should begin by taking from yourself.*

So, firstly, as it says, we should meditate on compassion by taking from sentient beings their sufferings and the causes of their sufferings. Begin by taking upon yourself all your own actions and disturbing emotions and the sufferings that you will have to experience as a result in future lives in any of the five or six states of existence. Imagine that these form black heaps, similar to trimmings of hair[39], upon your present mental and physical aggregates[40] and think that you are thereby freed from these sufferings and their causes in all future lives. Similarly, imagine that you accept the sufferings and sources of suffering of tomorrow, the day after that, the coming months and years and the rest of your life upon your present temporary aggregates of today, this month and this year, and think that you thereby free yourself from all misery from tomorrow onwards.

In taking all the sufferings of others upon yourself, you should not keep them in some inconspicuous place, but in your heart, since the very purpose of accepting them is to eradicate your self-centred attitude. As explained during the meditation on love, you should accept all the originating and resultant sufferings of the denizens of hell at your heart like heaps of black hair trimmings. Think that your selfish attitude is mellowed and subdued and that the denizens of hell are freed of all sufferings without exception.

In a similar way take on the originating and resultant sufferings of all the hungry spirits, animals, and human beings of the four continents and the eight sub-continents, the six categories of gods of desire, such as the gods of the four great kings, the twelve categories of gods of form, from the Brahma Family to the Great Result and the beings of the four states of the formless realm, from all the worldly realms throughout the ten directions, no matter how many there are. Imagine that all these originating and resultant sufferings fall, as if shaved off with a razor, onto your heart, that your self-centred attitude is mellowed and subdued, and that sentient beings are freed of all sufferings and their causes without exception. Likewise, apply the same mode of thought by taking on the miseries of the beings of the intermediate state.

It is worthwhile to think briefly of taking on each and every suffering distinctly, in general and in particular, as well as their origins in actions and disturbing emotions, from all sentient beings of the four kinds of birth and to think of freeing them from them. Since the Hearers and Solitary Realisers abiding on any of the five paths, and practitioners of the great vehicle below the path of meditation, possess slight sufferings and their origins, the manner of taking these on is as before. There is nothing to be taken from the hearts of the Buddhas, nor from our own spiritual masters, for we are taught to identify them with the Buddhas.

TAKING (UNSATISFACTORINESS) FROM THE ENVIRONMENT (WHICH BEINGS INHABIT)

Think that all the impure realms within the ten directions, which are the products of actions and disturbing emotions, are transformed into pure worlds. Geshey Sha-wo-pa remarked that this doctrine of training in love and compassion by way of taking all sufferings and their origins upon yourself and providing others with every happiness and virtue is a practice for banishing fear. Should you wonder about the source of these practices, they can be traced to the *Biography of Manibhadra* in the *Buddhāvatamsaka Sutra*, which says,

> Imagine transferring the suffering of sentient beings onto yourself and transforming the self into the body that sustains them.

The *Prayers of Supreme Conduct* also say,

> May all the heaps of sufferings of wandering beings
> The sufferings of hell beings, animals and spirits,
> Those of human beings, gods and anti-gods,
> Fall on me and may they find bliss.

Moreover, the *Prayers for Granting Supreme Love* say,

> May the gods, anti-gods and great serpents
> Of all the innumerable worlds, from the Peak
> Of Existence above to the Hell Without Respite below,
> Find happiness as I take on their suffering.

The master Nāgārjuna says,

> May their unwholesome deeds bear fruit for me
> And may my virtues bear fruit for them.

Shāntideva says,

> Equalise yourself and others
> Then exchange yourself with others.

And,

> Having seen the faults of self-centredness
> And the ocean of good in (concern for) others,
> I shall completely give up all selfishness,
> And accustom myself to accepting others.

And,

> Whoever is keen to give swift protection
> To both himself and others
> Should practise the sublime secret
> Of equalising and exchanging self and others.

And,

> If you do not actually exchange your happiness
> For the sufferings of others,
> You will not become enlightened

Nor find any joy in cyclic existence.

And,

Therefore, in order to allay harm to yourself
And pacify the pains of others,
Offer yourself in the service of others
And protect them as you would yourself.

And,

Whatever the agonies of sentient beings may be,
May they all ripen on me alone.

The *Ornament of Great Vehicle Sutras* says,

Finding the mind that equalises self and others
Or values others more than self is good,
Thus, it is taught that others' welfare is superior to one's own.

The *Seventy Prayers* say,

I would not mind being thrown
Into any of the hells as a result
Of the slightest misdeed by sentient beings
Who are afflicted by poisonous disturbing emotions.

Whatever the agonies of beings may be,
I volunteer to accept them all.

May they always engage in virtue
And be satisfied by supreme happiness.

The *Special Verses Collected by Topic* say,

Your body and your life
Should be given to all sentient beings.
Love and compassion should be given
Equally to all living creatures.

Earnestly wishing all evil

To ripen upon your mindstream,
Rejoice in all merits
And think of the great being, the Buddha.

And,

You should give away your body
Life and mind.

And,

Let all the misdeeds of
All living beings ripen on me.
By accepting all their misdeeds,
May these beings avoid suffering

And,

Make others' (sufferings) your own
And give your own (happiness) to others.

The regular confession of Samvara's ritual also says,

May the miseries of all sentient beings mature on me
May they enjoy happiness due to my virtues.
In all my lives may my three doors be transformed
Into the excellent vase and the wish-granting tree.

So, this is what is taught in many of the great vehicle texts containing the Buddha's words and commentaries to them. But should you wonder whether there are not those who belong definitely and ultimately to the lineages of Hearers and Solitary Realisers, and if so how it could be possible for all sentient beings to become Buddhas—you should know that the presentation of three vehicles is interpretable for temporary purposes, whereas in the ultimate and definitive sense there is only one vehicle. The *Expression of the Names of Mañjushrī* says,

The result of the one vehicle is present
In the three vehicles' determination to be free.

There are many such quotations in the great vehicle.

Having familiarised yourself with giving and taking to some extent, the way to practise it concisely is as follows. The text says,

These two should be made to ride on the breath

When you have acquired some training in the preceding process, as you exhale imagine that you are giving your body, possessions, and virtues of the three times to all sentient beings under the sky and that they thereby obtain ultimate and uncontaminated bliss. As you inhale you should imagine you are taking into your heart all the sufferings of every being in the three realms, as well as their causes, and that they are thereby completely freed from all misery and its causes. Practising in this way the mind and breath will flow in the same direction, so you will overcome distraction and strengthen mindfulness.

THE PRACTICE TO BE FOLLOWED IN THE PERIODS AFTER AND IN BETWEEN MEDITATION SESSIONS

Concerning the three objects, three poisons and three virtues
The instruction to be followed, in brief,
Is to take these words to heart in all activities.

When the six senses come into contact with the six objects, such as those that are attractive, unattractive and neutral, if the three corresponding poisonous or disturbing emotions arise, sincerely train your mind. Think, 'By these means I have cut off all the disturbing emotions of all the many beings overpowered by them in this world. May they thus abide in virtue and be freed from the three poisons.' Practise this in all activities, whether standing, strolling, lying or sitting, and at all times whether day or night. Just as Kamalashīla's *Stages of Meditation* says,

The great compassionate one, in all his actions, whether

walking or standing, and at all times, must acquaint himself with all sentient beings. Such a thought should be complemented by reciting the following lines,

> May their misdeeds ripen on me
> And may all my virtues ripen on them.
> May all sentient beings' sufferings mature on me
> And through my virtues may they all be happy.
> Whatever agonies beings may suffer
> May they ripen on me alone.
> Through all the virtues of Bodhisattvas
> May wandering beings enjoy bliss.

This must be practised from the depth of your heart. The great Sha-ra-wa said,

> You can train and accustom yourself to this instruction of mine, neither in the manner of a single long beam, no matter how level or extended it may be, nor like a stone rolling down a rugged hill-side, no matter how tough, nor like stagnant lukewarm pond water. But if you strive with absolute determination, as the saying goes, 'Red as blood and white as curd,' then like a donkey emerging from a flock of sheep, you will be freed from all interferences and sufferings. If you hesitate over whether it is proper or improper, or whether you can or cannot engage in the training, it will not be successful.

The method of exchanging self and others is equivalent to the first three points of the seven point cause and result training in the awakening mind[41], such as recognising beings as having been our mothers. The special wish has not been dealt with separately, since it is integral to the actual training in love and compassion within the practice of giving and taking.

THE PROCESS OF CULTIVATING THE AWAKENED MIND CONCERNED WITH ATTAINING THE FULLY AWAKENED STATE OF BEING

You might wonder what practical use love and compassion could be. Great beings like the Hearers, Solitary Realisers and great Bodhisattvas on the tenth stage possess boundless virtues enabling them to work for the welfare of other beings. Nevertheless, only by attaining the state of enlightenment can they place innumerable beings in the state beyond suffering, spontaneously and uninterruptedly until the end of cyclic existence, by emitting one ray of light or giving one session of discourse. In addition, it is only as a Buddha that you acquire perfection of your own personal fulfilment of abandonment and insight. Understanding this you should train yourself, thinking, 'I shall attain enlightenment to fulfil the aims of both myself and all sentient beings.' The benefits and advantages of training in the awakening mind in this way can be found in the *Questions of Viradutta Sutra*,

> If the merit of (generating) the awakening mind
> Were to take physical form,
> It would fill the whole of space
> And still exceed that.
>
> Were someone to fill the Buddha fields
> With the most precious jewels,
> Numerous as sand grains in the Ganges,
> And offered them to the Protector of the World,
>
> And were someone else simply to fold his hands
> Out of respect for the awakening mind,
> This latter would be the superior offering
> And its merit would be boundless.

The *Compendium of Training* says,

> The aspiration for the awakening mind is the resolution to become enlightened. So, this mind is attained by wishing for it.

This is how it is explained.

INSTRUCTIONS CONCERNING THE FIVE PRECEPTS THAT ARE FACTORS OF THE TRAINING

(a) Transforming adverse circumstances into the path
(b) The integrated practice of a single lifetime
(c) The measure of having trained the mind
(d) The commitments of mind training
(e) The precepts of mind training

TRANSFORMING ADVERSE CIRCUMSTANCES INTO THE PATH

This has two parts, the brief and the elaborate explanations. The text says,

> *When the environment and its inhabitants overflow with unwholesomeness*
> *Transform adverse circumstances into the path to enlightenment.*

The environment is filled with the circumstantial results of the ten unwholesome actions and the sentient beings who inhabit it think of nothing but disturbing emotions and do nothing but unwholesome deeds. For these reasons, the gods, nāgas and hungry spirits, who favour such black actions, are invigorated and increase in their power and strength. As a result spiritual practitioners in general are troubled by many interferences, and those who have entered the door of the great vehicle are beset by various adverse factors. Under such circumstances, if you engage in this kind of practice and are able to transform hostile influences into conducive factors, to see opponents as supporters and harmful elements as spiritual friends, you will be able to use adverse conditions as supporting factors in the achievement of enlightenment. In this context Geshey Chen-nga-wa said to Geshey Sha-wo-pa, 'It is amazing that your disciples of mind training take support from adverse factors and experience sufferings as happiness'.

The elaborate explanation has two parts: taking adverse circumstances into the path of enlightenment by relying on the special thought of the awakening mind, and by relying on the excellent practices of accumulation and purification.

TAKING ADVERSE CIRCUMSTANCES INTO THE PATH BY RELYING ON THE SPECIAL THOUGHT OF THE AWAKENING MIND

The text says,

Apply meditation immediately at every opportunity

We should take lightly every mental or physical difficulty that befalls us, be it great, moderate or slight, whatever the circumstances, in happy times or hard times, whether we are at home or in a foreign country, in a village or a monastery, in the company of human or non-human friends. We should think of the many kinds of sentient beings in the boundless universe afflicted with similar troubles and make prayers that our own sufferings may serve as a substitute for theirs and that they may be parted from all misery. Considering how wonderful it is to have fulfilled the purpose of our practice of compassion by taking on the suffering of others, we should sincerely rejoice.

When we enjoy happiness and prosperity and suffer no lack of food, clothing, dwelling, friends or spiritual masters, but possess these external conditions in abundance, and when, suffering no internal problems, such as sudden discomfort caused by mental or physical sickness, we are able to put our faith and so on into practice, we should recognise that all these favourable conditions for following an uninterrupted great vehicle practice, in these hard times when the teaching is degenerating, are the fruit of merits accumulated in the past. Therefore, it is essential to endeavour to accumulate merits on the basis of pure ethics, so as to obtain such uninterrupted prosperity in future lives. Those who cannot see the point of this, due to their having obtained even a little wealth are, in many cases, governed by pride, arrogance and disdain. When they encounter even the slightest mental or physical trouble, they become discouraged, despondent and defeatist. We are taught not to behave like this, but to be undisturbed whether we encounter happiness or suffering.

TAKING ADVERSE CIRCUMSTANCES INTO THE PATH BY RELYING ON THE EXCELLENT PRACTICES OF ACCUMULATION AND PURIFICATION

The text says,

> *The supreme method is accompanied by the four practices*

(i) Accumulation of merit

If you dislike suffering and wish for peace, thinking that it is easy to accumulate small, medium and large (virtues) in relation to the higher and lower fields of merit, do it in company with all sentient beings. The *Prayers of the Meditator Vidyujjvāla* say,

> Whatever is meant for my purpose
> Happiness or suffering, good or bad,
> May I accept it all.

(ii) Purification of negativity

All the misdeeds you have committed, or caused to be committed, over beginningless time due to the disturbing emotions, must be confessed repeatedly through the four powers.

(iii) Making offerings to evil spirits

As explained earlier in the context of thinking about the kindness of hostile forces, acquaint yourself with love, compassion and patience specifically towards them.

(iv) Offering ritual cakes to religious protectors and seeking their help

Arrange as many clean ritual cakes as you can afford and, visualising them as the most magnificent and extensive offerings, offer them to the religious protectors you have invoked through the prescribed ritual. You should pray from the depths of your heart,

> 'May I be able to see adverse circumstances as the path to enlightenment, as the holy Buddhas and Bodhisattvas of the past have done. And just as the precious awakening mind, which is the core of the general body of the teachings of the great vehicle, was born in the mindstreams of the holy ones of the past, may I generate, maintain, and increase it my mindstream. And may I be granted your virtuous help so that I may be able to benefit sentient beings through body, speech and mind whenever I see, hear, think or come into contact with them.'

THE INTEGRATED PRACTICE OF A SINGLE LIFETIME

The text says,

> *Train in the five powers*

(i) The power of intention

We must set a strong determination, thinking, 'I shall not let the primary or secondary disturbing emotions, which arise from the misconception of self, dominate my activities of body and speech even for a moment, from now until I attain enlightenment, or at any time in this life until I die, this year, this month, and today in particular.' Similarly, make a strong resolve thinking, 'I will become familiar with and never be separated from the awakening mind until I have attained the highest enlightenment, and so forth, and today in particular I shall not be parted from it.' The *King of Meditative Stabilisations Sutra* says,

> The more a human being analyses (something)
> Because the force of his thought is focused on it
> His mind dwells on it more strongly.

(ii) The power of the white seed

We need to preserve the merits and insights arising from generosity, ethics, and meditation, which cause us to generate, maintain and enhance the precious awakening mind.

(iii) The power of remorse

Understanding their disadvantages, as were explained earlier in the context of exchanging self and others, we should try to give up such disturbing emotions as the misconception of self, the self-centred attitude it gives rise to, and the inclination to neglect others, by means of regret. We should follow the training advised in the *Guide to the Bodhisattva's Way of Life which* says,

> It would be better for me to be burned,
> To have my head cut off, and be killed,
> Than ever bowing down to my enemies,
> The ubiquitous disturbing emotions

(iv) The power of prayer

We should make great prayers that by the force of mundane and transcendental merit in general, and especially our own merit created by body, speech and mind throughout the three times, all sentient beings in general, and ourselves in particular, may generate the awakening mind that they have not generated, and that it may abide and thrive in those who have.

(v) The power of acquaintance

We should familiarise ourselves at all times and in all circumstances solely with the actual meditations as they were explained above. The *Guide to the Bodhisattva's Way of Life* says,

> The childish work for their own benefit,
> The Buddhas work for the welfare of others,
> Just look at the difference between them.

If we familiarise ourselves with this practice and maintain the conditions for doing so, we will gain perfection, as the saying goes,

> There is nothing that does not become easier with acquaintance.

The great Che-ka-wa said,

> This mind that is full of faults
> Has one great quality,
> That it does whatever it is taught.

APPLYING THE FIVE POWERS AT THE TIME OF DEATH

In relating these instructions on the five powers to the advice concerning what to do at the time of death, the text says,

> *The five powers themselves are the great vehicle's*
> *Precept on the transference of consciousness,*
> *Cultivate these paths of practice.*

(i) The power of the white seed

We should purify the misdeeds which will cause us suffering in the future, by application of the four powers. At the time of death be fearless and free from sorrow, thinking, 'It's all right for me die.' It is extremely important not to hold onto anything that will be a source of attachment, but to offer all your possessions to the higher and lower fields of merit. There are many (examples of) incidents such as that concerning the Bhikṣhu, whose body burned thrice simultaneously due to his attachment to his alms bowl at the time of death[42]. We should especially eliminate attachment to our bodies at the time of death. This is because the body has been the basis of the 'I', or misconception of self, the root of all disturbing emotions, wherever we have been born in all the six realms of existence. And being attached to the body, we have indulged in the ten unwholesome deeds, the five boundless actions and other deleterious behaviour, in order to obtain food, clothing and other possessions to meet our own selfish ends. Consequently, we are submerged in the unending sufferings of cyclic existence in general and the unbearable pains of inferior rebirths in particular. As the *Guide to the Bodhisattva's Way of Life* says,

> Whoever is attached to this body
> Is frightened by even small things.
> Who would not despise as his enemy
> A body which gives rise to such fear?
>
> Wishing to find a means to relieve
> This body's hunger, thirst, and sickness,
> You kill birds, fish and deer
> And loiter by the roadside to rob others.
>
> If, for the sake of profit and comfort
> You would even kill your father and mother
> And misappropriate offerings to the Three Jewels,
> You will burn in the most severe hell.
>
> What wise man would desire, protect
> And coddle this body?
> Who would not scorn it and
> Regard it as an enemy?

So, we should make a strong determination not adopt such an inferior body, the product of actions and disturbing emotions, in the future, but to let the reality of the mind, its lack of inherent existence, rest in the perfect body of truth.

(ii) The power of intention

As explained above, we should have three types of intention, related to the long, medium and short terms.

(iii) The power of remorse

Remembering the disadvantages of the disturbing emotions, we should protect ourselves from being overwhelmed by them.

(iv) The power of prayer

We should make strong prayers never to be separated from the awakening mind under any circumstances, nor to be dominated by the misconception of self or the disturbing emotions.

(v) The power of familiarity

This concerns physical actions, such as lying on your right side, your right cheek resting on your right hand, your head pointing to the north with your ring finger stopping the breath from your right nostril, and your left hand on your left thigh. Breathing only through your left nostril, transfer your consciousness. In this context the great Che-ka-wa said,

> There are many marvellous instructions on the transference of consciousness, but this is the most wonderful of them all.

THE MEASURE OF HAVING TRAINED THE MIND

The text says,

> *Integrate all the teachings into one thought*

Since all the Buddha's teachings and the commentaries to them were meant to subdue the misconception of self, and since that is the conception that is to be eradicated or exhausted, we should examine whether the activities of our body, speech and mind favour and encourage the misconception of self or oppose it. If we find that they favour the it, then we have missed the point of hearing, contemplating and meditating on the doctrine. If, however, they oppose it, that is a sign of a successful practice of the doctrine and that we have engaged in authentic mind training. This is the scale against which the practitioner should be weighed. We should ensure that we are not disappointed when subjected to such assessment. The text says,

Primary importance should be given to the two witnesses

Other people may also serve as witnesses, commenting that you are engaging in proper practice and that your mind has become smooth and cool, but this is of no help. The vitally important thing is that when we examine ourselves, under any circumstances, we should see that we are not deceiving, fooling, or embarrassing ourselves. If we have trained our minds with regard to the most unpleasant worldly phenomena and achieve what we desire, this shows that we have trained our minds.

The text says,

Constantly cultivate only a joyful mind

Having experienced the flavour of the teaching through meditation, whatever adverse conditions such as suffering and ill-repute may arise, if your meditation is unaffected by such discouraging conditions, and you only generate happiness and rejoicing, thinking, 'The practice of mind training through giving and taking has been meaningful,' then the counteracting forces have been initially effective. In brief, it is a great mistake to destroy your virtue through anger that rankles over slight hardships encountered in the course of mind training. The great Sha-wo-pa said,

There is no worse form of abuse than to say that your spiritual friend has no peace of mind.

Regarding the actual measure of a trained mind, the text says,

The measure of a trained mind is that it has turned away

This refers to the arising of an experience of the stages of practice in your mind, from contemplation of the preliminary practices up to the training in the ultimate awakening mind, so that an awareness of the need to make the most of freedom and opportunity under all circumstances, without wasting them, arises naturally in the mind.

SIGNS OF TRAINED MIND

The text says,

There are five great marks of a trained mind.

1. The great hero, who constantly familiarises himself with the awakening mind in the knowledge that it is the essence of all the teachings.
2. The great disciplinarian, who is careful to avoid even the slightest offence out of his conviction in the law of cause and effect.
3. The great ascetic, who can bear hardships in the course of subduing the disturbing emotions in his mind.
4. The great practitioner of virtue, who never separates the activities of his body and speech from the tenfold conduct of the great vehicle.
5. The great yogi, who constantly practises the yoga of the awakening mind and its associated teachings.

The text says,

The trained (mind) retains control even when distracted

Just as a skilled rider will not fall if his horse bolts while he is distracted, similarly, even if we inadvertently hear unpleasant remarks, such as accusations from hostile quarters, or we are criticised and mocked, as there are many who even criticise Buddha, the Transcendent Subduer, we should understand that it is undoubtedly the result of negative actions we have committed.

Whoever criticises me,
Or inflicts harm upon others,
Or similarly ridicules me,
May they be blessed with enlightenment.

When such a thought (as expressed in the *Guide to the Bodhisattva's Way of Life*) arises naturally in your heart, that is a sign of having trained the mind.

THE IRREVERSIBLE COMMITMENTS OF MIND TRAINING

This has two parts: the explanation of what appears in the text in verse and of what appears in the text as maxims.

EXPLANATION OF WHAT APPEARS IN THE TEXT IN VERSE

The text says,

Always train in the three general points

These are as follows: mind training that is not contrary to the commitments, which is not led astray, and which is impartial.

Firstly, we should never act in contradiction to the practices common to all vehicles, saying, 'There's no harm in this because I'm training the mind,' when we break some minor commitment, claiming that nothing else is required of a follower of mind training. On the contrary, we should train in practising the Buddha's teaching in its entirety from the instruction on basic logic up to the Guhyasamāja Tantra.

Secondly, we should avoid digging harmful earth, felling sinister trees, stirring noxious waters, visiting those afflicted by contagious diseases without precaution or associating by view or behaviour with those who are morally corrupt or possessed by spirits. We should follow the pure and unbroken tradition descending from the great Atīsha, the sole divine lord, to the all-knowing Tsong-kha-pa and his disciples.

Thirdly, we should be impartial about the object of our mind training, whether it is human or inhuman; friend, foe or stranger; superior, inferior or equal; or high, middling or low. This is because we should practise compassion without distinction towards all sentient beings under the sky. Given that the disturbing emotions in our mindstreams, the objects to be abandoned, are to be subdued, it is not sufficient to apply a partial or alternative remedy. We should train in understanding the way the antidotes are to be applied in general, without partiality to the disturbing emotions. This is because all these disturbing emotions are obstructions to liberation and omniscience and are equal in dragging us into the miseries of cyclic existence. So, we need to be impartial if we are to have an unbiased attitude towards all.

The text says,

Engage vigorously in forceful cultivation and abandonment

In general, we are not supposed to employ force towards human or inhuman beings, because it will provoke their anger and the inhuman beings, holding a grudge, will harm us in this and future lives, as well as in the intermediate state. Amongst human beings we should not behave forcefully towards those who have been kind to us, or even towards our relatives and servants, otherwise the help they have previously given us will become worthless and a cause for anger. Towards whom then should we be forceful? In general, all the faults of cyclic existence arise from its origin, actions and disturbing emotions, and actions are produced because of disturbing emotions. Since, among all disturbing emotions, the misconception of self is chief, all our spiritual practices of hearing, contemplation and meditation involving our body, speech and mind, should be concentrated forcefully on eliminating it. With regard to the method by which to do this, The *Guide to the Bodhisattva's Way of Life* says,

> To do this will be my sole obsession.
> Holding a strong grudge I shall meet them in battle,
> So, here a disturbing emotion can destroy
> Other disturbing emotions, but not otherwise.
>
> It would be better for me to be burned,
> To have my head cut off, and be killed,
> Than ever bowing down to my enemies,
> The ubiquitous disturbing emotions.

So, we must persevere in combatting the misconception of self and familiarising ourselves with concern for others.

Regarding what we must do to give up our self-centred attitude, the text says,

> *Subjugate all the reasons (for selfishness).*

We should suppress every instance of attachment and hatred that gives rise to exaggerated prejudices about friends, foes, or strangers, the attractive and unattractive. This is because worldly phenomena in general are unreliable and relations between friends and foes in particular are uncertain. (As the *Friendly Letter* says,)

> Your father becomes your son, your mother your wife,
> And your enemies become friends.
> The opposite also takes place. Therefore,
> In cyclic existence there is no certainty at all.

There is also a saying,

> Construct a fort where the danger is greatest.

It is necessary to meditate on the factors which cause your spiritual practice to decline. The text says,

> *Train consistently to deal with difficult situations*

FIVE KINDS OF DIFFICULT SITUATION

Firstly, since even slight misbehaviour towards the Three Jewels, your abbot, spiritual master, parents and so forth, who are all very kind to you, is extremely serious, you should be careful not to lose your temper with them.

Secondly, as there are many opportunities for disturbing emotions to arise in relation to the members of your family, because you live with them all the time, this requires special training.

Thirdly, you should train yourself particularly in relation to everyone, whether an ordained or lay-person, who appears to be your rival, otherwise when even a small misfortune befalls them it may create satisfaction in your heart.

Fourthly, you should make a point of training yourself in relation to those who accuse you when you have done nothing against them, because there is a risk that, as the saying goes, 'If the fire of hatred burns, the moisture of compassion will dry up.'

Fifthly, you should pay special attention in your meditation to those people the mere sight of whom, or the mere sound of whose names, you dislike, even though they have done nothing against you. Because of this, there is a great danger of becoming angry with them.

In order to acquire equanimity towards such people, the text says,

Don't rely on other conditions

In general, whatever you are practising such as listening or contemplation, if favourable conditions are assembled it will be successful, and if the conditions are not met it will fail. Yet, if someone, who enters into this practice and engages sincerely in mind training, is able to see the lack of favourable conditions as a stepping stone, he will have no fear of external or internal obstacles and will make great advancement towards the awakening mind.

It is clear that you need steadfast behaviour in the course of your practice, as the text says,

Transform your attitude but maintain your natural behaviour

At no time should your thoughts be separated from becoming acquainted with the awakening mind. There should be no sudden change in your physical and verbal conduct and your behaviour should not differ from that of ordinary people. The great Che-ka-wa said that all our practices of mind training should be inconspicuous to the outside world, but in reality there should be great improvement.

When you have entered into the practice of mind training, you should not criticise or point out other people's faults. The text says,

Don't speak of others' incomplete qualities

You should give up criticising human and inhuman beings out of spite and should not point out their mistakes. The text says,

Don't concern yourself with others' business

You should neither think nor say such things as, 'I am able to cope because I am a practitioner of mind training, otherwise it would be impossible to deal with such a person.'

The fruits of your meditation should not be polluted with self-interest. The text says,

Give up every hope of reward

You should not expect any mundane prosperity in this life or future lives as a result of your meditation, nor should you seek the states of liberation and omniscience out of self-interest. This is because the state of enlightenment should be sought in the interest of sentient beings. (*Ornament for Clear Realisation* says,)

> The awakening mind is generated for others' welfare,
> The wish is for perfectly accomplished enlightenment.

EXPLANATION OF WHAT APPEARS IN THE TEXT AS MAXIMS

Avoid poisonous food

Generally, good food nourishes the body, but if it is poisoned, it can cause death. Similarly, the state of enlightenment springs from listening, contemplation and so forth, but if they are polluted by misconceptions such as the eight worldly concerns and selfish thoughts of I and mine, they can take the life of liberation and omniscience. So, please don't let whatever merit you acquire be sullied by them.

Don't maintain inverted loyalty

This refers to holding a grudge against people for some small wrong they have done you and retaliating angrily. You should never indulge in such behaviour or every chance of generating love and compassion towards them will be destroyed.

Don't make malicious banter

Do not speak abusively in a way that strikes at the heart of anyone who hears it. The esteemed Che-ka-wa explains this as saying such things as, 'At the time you committed that offence, I did not respond,' 'It is not clear whether this has been done or not,' and so forth. Pouring out a string of such invective will ruin the seeds of your practice.

Don't wait in ambush

This refers to nursing a grudge against someone for some slight and retaliating when you are in a position to do so. Once you have entered into this practice (of mind training), you cannot behave in such a fashion, since to do so would completely contradict the practice of taking others' troubles and sufferings upon yourself.

Don't strike at the vital point

This is to reveal others' mistakes out of spite. You should never do this to human or inhuman beings because it can provoke such severe anxiety as to cause death.

Don't place the load of a horse on a pony[43]

This refers to slyly avoiding a common problem and passing the unwanted burden to others.

Don't sprint to win the race

This is to try to take credit for some favour you have rendered in common with others, with expectation of receiving some sort of gratitude. As explained above a practitioner of mind training should not behave in such a manner.

Don't turn gods into devils

Just as you can lose your life if you make mistakes in the process of cultivating worldly gods, which is known as gods turning into devils, so, once you have entered into the practice of mind training, if any aspect of your listening, contemplation and meditation provokes your misconception of self and serves to increase it, it is known as turning gods into devils. Please see that this does not happen.

Don't seek others' misery as a means to happiness

This refers to waiting to capitalise on others' misfortune. You should train yourself never to act in such a fashion.

These are the commitments that a practitioner of mind training should never transgress.

THE PRECEPTS OF MIND TRAINING

This has two parts: the explanation of what appears in the text in verse and of what appears in the text in maxims.

EXPLANATION OF WHAT APPEARS IN THE TEXT IN VERSE

Every yoga should be performed as one

Ensure that yogas of all such activities as eating, dressing and residing are assimilated into the single practice of training the mind.

There are two activities at both beginning and end

Just as explained above concerning the power of intention, you should set a strong resolve to eliminate unwholesome activities and acquire their antidotes. You should do this when you wake every morning throughout your life. When you go to sleep at night, if you find that the behaviour of your body and speech has been in accord with your resolve, you can rejoice, thinking that your having found life as a free and fortunate human being, met with the teaching of the great vehicle and come under the care of spiritual masters has been worthwhile. But, if you have not done as you had resolved, reflecting that you have worthlessly wasted your leisure and opportunities and that your meeting with the profound teaching has been without purpose, determine not to do the same in future.

Train first in the easier practices

If you feel that it is difficult to take on the miseries of others and to give away your own happiness and merits, recall that at present you are training in these practices only on a mental level. When, due to acquaintance, you have gained prowess, actually engaging in giving and taking will not be difficult.

Whichever occurs be patient with both

Whether happiness or suffering befalls the body and mind, as was explained in the context of transforming adverse conditions into the path, you should transform it into a factor conducive to accomplishing enlightenment.

Guard both at the cost of your life

The pledged or natural commitments of the three vows you have taken, and, in particular, the commitments of mind training explained above, should be guarded even at the cost of your life.

Train in the three difficulties

In the first place it is hard to remember the remedies for the disturbing emotions, secondly, it is difficult to oppose them and thirdly, it is difficult to cut their continuity. Therefore, recognising the disturbing emotions and mindful of their disadvantages make efforts through various means to dispel them and put an end to the sequence.

Transform everything into the great vehicle path

All your actions should be accompanied by love and compassion for all sentient beings and consequent interest in their enlightenment, so that until the end of cyclic existence the actions of your body, speech and mind, as well as seeing, hearing, remembering and contact can be transformed into the path of the great vehicle. *Birth Stories* says,

> Whether seeing, hearing, remembering, meeting or talking to them, always do whatever will be beneficial for sentient beings and will bring them peace.

And in the words of the esteemed Che-ka-wa,

> May all those who see me become enlightened and may everyone who comes into contact with me and talks with me consequently reach the state of enlightenment without obstruction.

This is the yoga on which to rely.

Value an encompassing and far-reaching practice

Training in the awakening mind also should not be biased towards just a few beings, but should indiscriminately encompass all beings of the four types of birth. It should not be disingenuous like a fisherman's visit to a temple, but practised sincerely from the depths of your heart. As Sha-wo-pa said,

> May they all ripen together collectively
> And may they all be worn out through grinding.

On his deathbed Che-ka-wa said, 'Se-chung-wa, I could not fulfil my wishes, but please place an offering to the Three Jewels on the altar.' When asked what his unfulfilled wishes had been, he said, 'I wished to experience the suffering of all sentient beings like a pall of black smoke over my heart, whereas I only experience a vision of the Blissful Land.'

Seek for the three principal causes

Whatever practice of hearing, contemplation, or meditation you do in general, particularly having entered the practice of mind training, if you possess the inner condition of life as a free and fortunate human being endowed with the good qualities of faith, discriminating awareness, effort and so forth, and the external condition of having formed a warm and honest relationship with a spiritual master[44], who is delighted to take care of you, under such circumstances, if you have access to such facilities as food and clothes in moderation, then it may turn out as did the meeting of the great Atīsha and Drom-tön-pa. Evidently, if you are missing one of these conditions, indicated by inadequate improvement in your understanding, you should endeavour to accumulate positive qualities as causes and pray that your knowledge will increase like the waxing moon.

Purify the coarser ones first

You must make an effort to counter all the disturbing emotions in general, and in particular the coarser ones, through a fine analysis of your mind.

Practise that which is more effective

In general, generosity is worthwhile, but observance of pure moral discipline is more powerful. Similarly, it is most important to lay the potential for the awakening mind and not to be separated from it under any circumstances.

Don't let three factors weaken

This refers to not letting your faith in and respect for your spiritual masters diminish, not letting your attention to ethical training waver, and not letting your joy in mind training lessen. If you do not believe in or respect your master, there is no way for you to develop knowledge, and if your concern for ethical training decreases, there is no chance for your ethics to be pure, for all downfalls and misdeeds come about through recklessness. If your interest in mind training declines, you will lack the faith that would enable you to appreciate the qualities of the awakening mind and the aspiration and so forth that are its result. The drawback of this is that lacking a heartfelt interest in the doctrine you will pay it only lip-service.

Never be parted from the three possessions

You should not cease to perform virtuous physical actions, such as acts of service towards your spiritual masters and the Three Jewels, prostration and circumambulation. You should not cease to recite the refuge formula or recitations pertaining to meditational deities with your speech and in your mind you should nurture and never be parted from the awakening mind and its associated practices.

If you relapse, meditate on it as the antidote

For some people, wrong meditation gives rise to such attitudes as, 'Having meditated on mind training, slanderous attacks have increased,' 'The misconception of self and other disturbing emotions have increased,' 'My resources, such as food and clothing have declined, and I'm troubled by an increase in sickness and the interference of evil spirits.' If you feel like this, you will lose interest in mind training and there is a risk of your giving up the practice. In such circumstances you should think, 'This practice will never deceive me, it is the influence of demons which is causing me to relapse from the practice of meditation.' Wish from the depth of your heart that for the many people in the world whose minds are turned away from the doctrine, this may serve as a cause for them to integrate their minds with the teachings of the great vehicle.

Engage in the principal practices right now

We have been deprived of freedom in inferior rebirths over beginningless time, but now due to certain inner and outer conditions we have found this life as a free and fortunate human being. At such a time it is more important to work to actualise the purposes of future lives than those of this life. Since practice is more important than study, I urge you to unify the focus of your meditation on the awakening mind and its associated precepts.

In future always put on armour

This refers to putting on the armour-like determination not to be separated from the awakening mind under any circumstances in the future, until you have attained Buddhahood. The *Cloud of Jewels Sutra* recommends the determination to acquaint yourself with the awakening mind and never to be separated from it as a cause of not being parted from it.

EXPLANATION OF WHAT APPEARS IN THE TEXT AS MAXIMS

Don't apply a wrong understanding

We should acquaint ourselves with compassion for sentient beings tormented by various sufferings, but to feel pity for those who are slightly troubled by lack of food or clothes as a result of their endeavouring to listen to and think about religion is inverted compassion. We need to set an intention to attain ultimate enlightenment for the sake of all living beings, but to do so out of interest in worldly prosperity in general and the rewards and honour of this life in particular is a perverse intention. We should have an intention to elevate all sentient beings to the state of a Buddha, but to involve ourselves in taking care of the property of the Three Jewels in general and the Spiritual Community in particular in the hope that they will befriend us is a perverse intention.

If, from the depth of your hearts, you admire all Buddhas' and Bodhisattvas' practice of virtue, your own source of virtue will increase many times over, but to rejoice over the small mishaps that befall someone you dislike is unseemly admiration. You should meditate on the patience that endures whatever small sufferings and hardships arise in the course of listening, thinking and meditating, that accepts whatever small hindrances occur, and does not retaliate however you may be harmed. But it is misplaced patience if instead you endure the various sufferings which result from subduing your foes and caring for your relatives and so forth motivated by the eight worldly concerns. Having entered the door of the great vehicle doctrine, you should experience the flavour of this holy teaching by hearing and contemplating it. But, on the contrary, to indulge in sensual pleasures and, motivated by attachment, to taste your enemy's defeat and your relatives' defence is to experience the wrong flavour. These things should be given up.

Don't be sporadic

This refers to meditating occasionally and performing some virtues of body and speech in the name of religion, but without wholehearted faith in the practice of mind training, being chiefly involved in amassing wealth for this life. Instead of behaving like this, it is appropriate to concentrate all activities of body, speech and mind single-pointedly on this practice (of mind training). This is because this is the sole path traversed by all the Buddhas of the three times.

Practise unflinchingly

This supports the previous point. Without wavering, integrate all aspirations to one purpose.

Release investigation and analysis

This means that you should give up gross and subtle analysis of your motivation for your actions of body, speech and mind with reference to your long, middling and short term aims and should spend the time rejoicing.

Don't be boastful

Do not boast of the little good you have done for others by repeatedly reminding them of it. If it were proper to boast of the good you have done, the Transcendent Subduer would have said so, but he didn't.

Don't be short-tempered

You should not express dissatisfaction with the size of offerings and rewards or you will breech the commitment not to grumble.

Don't make a short-lived attempt

It serves no purpose if you affect some effort in meditation at the beginning and then leave it altogether. Effort needs to be like a great river, or a strong bow string. The *Praise of the Praiseworthy* says,

> For you to prove your superiority
> Show neither flexibility nor rigidity,
> Therefore, your supreme quality
> Is to show no distinction of rank or partiality

Don't expect gratitude

This refers to not expecting an immediate reward for whatever little good you do. You should give up saying that there is no use being good or otherwise to such and such a person, because he can't even say thank you. The great Bodhisattva

Che-ka-wa put this into practice to good effect. With a sense of satisfaction he said,

> My manifold aspirations have given rise
> To humiliating criticism and suffering,
> But, having received instructions for taming the
> misconception of self,
> Even if I die I have no regrets.

This concludes the explanation of the training in the conventional awakening mind.

CULTIVATING THE ULTIMATE AWAKENING MIND

In training in cultivating the ultimate awakening mind there are (three factors), the type of person to whom the instructions should be given, the time for imparting the teachings, and the actual instructions on cultivating the ultimate awakening mind.

The type of person to whom the instructions should be given

First of all, these teachings should be given to someone who possesses the qualities of a suitable recipient, to do so otherwise would be the cause of a transgression (for both the teacher and the disciple). If you wonder how you can tell who has the qualities of a suitable vessel, Chandrakīrti's *Supplement to (Nāgārjuna's) Treatise on the Middle Way* says,

> Just as from (seeing) smoke you know there's fire
> And from (seeing) water fowl you know there's a lake,
> So, from observing his characteristics you will know
> The lineage of one having the mind of a Bodhisattva.

So, you will be able to gauge (suitability) from external physical and verbal signs. But what would these signs be like? If, when hearing instructions on emptiness for the first time, you feel a pleasure, joy and rapture that gives rise to such physical symptoms as the bristling of your hair and tears welling up in your eyes, these are unmistakable signs. The *Supplement to (Nāgārjuna's) Treatise on the Middle Way* says,

> When an ordinary being, on hearing about emptiness,
> Feels great joy arising repeatedly within him,

And due to such joy tears moisten his eyes
And the hair on his body stands up
He has in his mind the seed of complete enlightenment,
And is a fit vessel for intimate teachings on emptiness.

If emptiness is taught to unsuitable recipients, some, fearful and without faith, will turn away from it. And if they abandon it, they reject the essence of the Transcendent Subduer's teachings and, due to their spurning the truth of that doctrine, they will wander endlessly through the realms of ongoing existence. Some, who have superficial faith, will mistake the meaning of emptiness and assume it means nonexistence. Due to such distorted thinking they will plummet over the precipice (created by) ignoring the specific consequences of positive and negative actions.

However, if these teachings are given to those characterised, as explained above, as suitable recipients, due to their faultless understanding of emptiness as conveying the meaning of dependent arising, their realisation of emptiness will become a totally pure path to liberation. This is because they will maintain all the aspects of the method side of practice, such as purely safeguarding their ethical discipline, which is what qualifies them as suitable candidates for taking the practice of hearing, contemplating and meditating on emptiness to heart. Similarly, the *Supplement* says,

They will always adopt pure ethics and observe them,
Will give out of generosity, will cultivate compassion
And will meditate on patience. Dedicating such virtue
Entirely to full awakening for the liberation of wandering beings,
They pay respect to accomplished Bodhisattvas.

THE TIME FOR IMPARTING THE TEACHINGS

The text says,

> *When stability has been attained, impart the secret teaching*

The way people of the great vehicle lineage generally venture into the spiritual path is that they initially stabilise their view of emptiness and subsequently engage in the aspects of practice concerning method. However, according to this tradition, you first deeply contemplate the four fundamental topics of the preliminary practices and then in the actual practice you become well acquainted with the awakening mind and its attributes, seeking the meaning of enlightenment in the interest of others. In this tradition it is only after you have stabilised your acquaintance with the aspects of method that the secret teaching concerning the cultivation of the ultimate awakening mind is imparted.

In the context of training in the ultimate awakening mind the text says,

> *Consider all phenomena as like dreams,*
> *Examine the nature of unborn awareness.*
> *The remedy itself is released in its own place,*
> *Place the essence of the path on the nature of the basis of all.*

The first line indicates the method for determining the lack of true existence of phenomena included amongst the objects that are apprehended (by the mind). The second refers to the technique for establishing the lack of true existence of the consciousness which apprehends things (in such a way), and the third line indicates the means for comprehending the lack of true existence even of yourself, the investigator. These are modes of carrying out analytical meditation. The last line refers to the process of safeguarding your meditative equipoise through meditation, free from laxity and excitement, on the meaning of what is not found by analysis.

The way to maintain (the view) outside the meditation session is indicated by the line,

In between meditation sessions, be like a conjurer.

(Just as a conjurer feels no attachment for the illusions he creates, a meditator, after rising from meditation on emptiness, has no attachment to appearances). This will be taught later.

These are no more, no less, than the techniques for meditating on the ultimate awakening mind according to the words of the great teacher, Che-ka-wa.

THE ACTUAL INSTRUCTIONS ON CULTIVATING THE ULTIMATE AWAKENING MIND

Buddha, the Transcendent Subduer, prophesied that the protector Nāgārjuna, his spiritual son (Āryadeva) and their followers, would establish the unmistaken definitive and interpretable meaning of emptiness as the essence of his teaching. Subsequently, Chandrakīrti established the meaning of selflessness. The great lord Atīsha concurred that he had faultlessly presented the intention of the Conqueror, saying,

> Who has realised emptiness?
> He who was prophesied by the One Thus Gone
> And saw the true reality,
> Nāgārjuna's disciple, Chandrakīrti.
> By following the instructions derived from him
> You will realise the true reality.

In accordance with that assertion and the thought of the King of the Doctrine, Tsong-kha-pa, emanation of the revered lord Mañjushrī, in whom the wisdom and compassion of all the Buddhas of the three times is brought together as one, there are two main outlines: recognising what ignorance is and how it is the source of cyclic existence; and showing that in order to eradicate it, we need to determine the view of selflessness and also to have a technique for doing so.

RECOGNISING WHAT IGNORANCE IS

Ignorance, or a lack of basic awareness, is diametrically opposed to awareness.[45] It is not merely other than awareness, nor is it the mere negation of awareness. It is the opposing factor that directly contradicts awareness. This awareness itself should not be understood as just any sort of awareness, but as the discriminating intelligence[46] that cognises the meaning of selflessness. That being the case, (ignorance) is that which exaggerates (phenomena), conceiving of them as being self-existent. This involves two kinds of misconception of self—that of persons and that of phenomena. The objects of these two are the objects of the mode of exaggeration projected onto persons and phenomena, that is, the self of persons and phenomena.

In addition, the most vital factor in determining selflessness is to ascertain the extent of the object of negation, so that neither too little nor too much is negated. If the object of negation is too extensive, existence and true existence will be mingled together as one, and since we accept that the mental projection, true existence, is what is to be negated, when, according to the system of refuting true existence, we perform the (actual) negation, we will not know how validly to establish existence. Instead we will present everything, such as the defiled and pure aspects of dependent arising, in a distorted way.

When those, who do not understand how to establish valid existence in their own system, engage in meditation on the established meaning of the view free of the two extremes, the basis of the path traversed by the Awakened Ones of the three times, they will be gravely confused in their presentation of the entirety of the grounds, paths and fruits. For at the resultant point of meditation on the inseparability of wisdom and method, when the Truth Body and Form Body are actualised in one person's mindstream, having one nature, yet distinct, he or she will act to benefit sentient beings spontaneously and unremittently until cyclic existence has been emptied.

If the object of negation is too narrow, although the principles of the four seals of Buddha's doctrine[47] are unanimously acknowledged by all Buddhist traditions as being literally what was spoken, when we set out to identify the self which does not exist, that is referred to by (the seal) 'all phenomena have no self', (we will see that) the Hearers do not assert a self of phenomena (as an object of negation), let alone the selflessness resulting from its negation. They take the selflessness of the (four) seals to be the mere selflessness of the person and that too as a person's being merely empty of being a self-sufficient, substantially existent entity.

For those great pioneers who propounded the system of 'mere awàreness' (the Mind Only school[48]) the seal concerning the non-existence of self implies the selflessness of both persons and phenomena. With respect to the latter, the self of phenomena is the distinct identity of the object and the perceiver, consequently, they assert that the lack of such identity is the selflessness of phenomena. The propounders of entitylessness (the Middle Way schools[49]) are of two types: the Consequentialists[50]and the Inherence Validators[51].

For the Inherence Validators, the seal stating 'the self is nonexistent' refers to the two selflessnesses. Their approach to the selflessness of the person is the same as the preceding two schools (the Mind Only school and the two Hearer traditions, the Particularists[52] and the Sutra Followers[53]). With regard to the selflessness of phenomena, since it is stated in the *Blaze of Reasoning* (by Bhāvaviveka, the Inherence Validator school's founder) that as all sensory consciousnesses, which, not being produced by fleeting or temporary causes of deception, take as their appearing objects things which exist due to their own characteristics, they assert inherent existence or existence due to its own characteristics posited by the force of a nonconceptual thought, which is unmistaken with regard to its appearing object, and conceptual thoughts unmistaken with regard to their referent objects. Because of this the self to be negated, or in other words that which does not exist in all phenomena, such as the aggregates, elements, sources and so forth, is that ultimate mode of existence which is not designated through the force of its appearance to an unmistaken consciousness. Consequently, negation of this is asserted to be the selflessness of phenomena.

Some earlier Tibetan masters asserted that the nonexistent self referred to in the Buddha's seal, 'all phenomena are selfless', can bear analysis by an analytical awareness examining the ultimate mode of being, which means the same as to say that it is established by that analytical awareness, that it holds its own in the face of that analytical awareness, and that it is the object of apprehension of that analytical awareness. If something is the object of apprehension of an analytical awareness examining the ultimate, it must necessarily be able to bear analysis. If that were so, they assumed it would have to be truly existent. Therefore, some said that it is not an object of an awareness analysing the ultimate, because if it were, there would be no basic object of negation. Thus, if it were an object of an analytical awareness examining the ultimate, it would have to bear analysis and if so, they say, it would have to be truly existent.

A number of Tibetan masters say that ultimate reality is truly existent because it is found by the awareness analysing the ultimate, since it is the object of that awareness. Some say that if ultimate truth were not an object of awareness it would be tantamount to underestimating ultimate truth. Thinking that if it were to become an object of valid awareness there would be no basic object of negation, they assert, from the viewpoint of this awareness, that although it has no perceivable object, from the perspective of inferential cognition the assembly of appearance and vacuity can still be said to be a perceivable object. Therefore, they say, the extremes of over-estimation and underestimation are avoided.

The Inherence Validators and all schools of tenets below assert no more than the presentation of disturbing emotions expounded in (Vasubandhu's own explanation of his) *Treasury of Knowledge*. Therefore, they all assert that the source of cyclic existence is intellectually acquired ignorance and the mistaken view of the transitory collection. However, intellectually acquired ignorance can be found only in those whose minds have been affected by the study of philosophy, therefore it cannot be the source of cyclic existence. The *Supplement* says,

> Even those who have spent many aeons as animals
> And have not beheld an unproduced or permanent (self),
> Are seen to be involved in the misconception of an 'I'.

If the object of intellectually acquired ignorance is taken as the measure for establishing the object of negation, the object of negation will be too narrow. Consequently, if we were to familiarise ourselves with the object to be realised through such negation, liberation would not occur, because the object of the mode of apprehension which conceives of persons, aggregates and so forth as existing by way of their own characteristics could not be dispelled. The *Precious Garland* says,

> So long as the aggregates are misconceived,
> An 'I' is misconceived upon them.
> If this conception of an 'I' exists,
> There is action which results in birth.

According to our own system there are two types of ignorance and that which acts as the root of cyclic existence is innate ignorance. But in terms of recognising its aspect and mode of apprehending the object, there are two kinds of people, those who do and those who do not understand the valid presentation of mere imputation by thought.

The outsiders (i.e. non-Buddhists) have no understanding of this and not all the schools of Buddhist tenets understand it. There are even two types among them, those who do and those who do not understand the presentation of functioning things, such as cause and effect and so forth. Even though all schools below the Inherence Validators assert the validity of those phenomena, they are unable to establish their validity when it concerns the meaning of mere designation of this or that by name. Therefore, they assert that if the object of a conventional imputation is found, they consider it to be validly established. If it is not found they consider it not to be validly established. Thus, they do not assert the validity of functional phenomena such as causation and production through mere imputation by thought.

Chandrakīrti's explanation of the thought of the Exalted Father (Nāgārjuna) and his son (Āryadeva) describes it as the most amazing exposition of the undistorted essence of the teaching of the Buddha, the Transcendent Subduer. It is able validly to establish causality and production, the perceived and the perceiver, the attainment and what gives rise to the attainment, through imputation by thought. Just as Nāgārjuna has said,

> Knowing that all phenomena are empty like this
> And relying upon actions and their results,
> Is a miracle amongst miracles,
> Is magnificent amidst magnificence.

The meaning of existence of its own accord, without being merely designated by force of thought to persons, aggregates and so forth, lies in all the object's marks of true existence, which are exaggerated by innate ignorance. When the basis for the negation of this is a person, it becomes the selflessness of a person. When the basis for the negation of this is the aggregates and so forth, it becomes the selflessness of phenomena. (Chandrakīrti's) *Commentary to (Āryadeva's) Four Hundred Verses* says,

> 'Self' here is that inherent existence of a phenomenon that is not dependent on others. The lack of this is selflessness. This should be understood according to the two categories, persons and phenomena, as the selflessness of persons and the selflessness of phenomena.

The way phenomena are designated by thought is stated in the *Questions of Upāli Sutra*,

> The variety of blooming flowers
> And the magnificent radiant golden castles
> Are not created by anyone,
> They are designated by thought,
> For the world is posited by the force of thought.

Thus, it explains that all phenomena are designated by the power of thought. *Sixty Stanzas of Reasoning* also says,

> If the Buddha rationally taught
> That the world is conditioned by ignorance,
> Why is it not appropriate
> To view the world as a misconception?

What this means is that worlds do not exist by their own nature, but by mere designation. *Four Hundred Verses* also says,

> If there is no (imputation by) thought,
> Even desire and so forth have no existence.
> Then, who with intelligence would maintain
> That a real object is (produced dependent on) thought.

The commentary adds,

> Undoubtedly, those that exist only through the existence of thought and those that do not exist when there is no thought are to be understood as not existing by way of their own entities, just as a snake is imputed to a coiled rope.

Therefore, from the viewpoint of imputation by thought, although lacking existence by way of their own nature, attachment and so forth are explained as being like a snake imputed to a (coiled) rope. There is not the slightest difference between the way phenomena such as persons like Devadatta and Yangdatta, or things like vases and woollen cloth are imputed by thought, and the way pebbles and sticks are designated as horses and elephants by a conjurer when he transforms them into such things, or the way a coiled rope at dusk is designated by thought as a snake. The rope mistaken for a snake is not merely designated by the force of a mistaken mind, in addition not the slightest fragment of a snake exists either in a part of the rope or in the coiled bundle. The same can be said of the conjurer's pebbles and sticks, reflections in a mirror and so forth.

An easier way of reaching a conviction about the way the innate misconception of self within our mindstreams gives rise to the misconception of a self of persons and phenomena is, as was explained before, that when a rope is mistaken for a snake, both the snake and the appearance of a snake in relation to the basis are merely projected by the force of a mistaken mind. Besides this, from the point of view of the rope, there is not the slightest trace of the existence of such an object (as a snake), which is merely projected by the mind. Similarly, when a face appears to be inside a mirror, even a canny old man knows that the appearance in the mirror of both the eyes, nose and so forth, and the reflection is merely a projection of a mistaken mind. Taking these as examples it easy to discern, easy to understand and easy to realise that there is not the slightest trace of existence from the side of the object itself.

In general, there are three kinds of apprehension involved in conceiving of the thought of an 'I'. Unlike the way a reflection appears to a canny old man, apprehending the object (the 'I') as though it exists due to its being established from its own side is the innate misconception of a self of persons. The object of such a mode of apprehension is the self of persons. The (mode of) apprehension that derives from exaggerating all compounded and uncompounded phenomena, from form up to the omniscient mind, is the innate misconception of a self of phenomena. The object of this mode of apprehension is the mark of true existence which is the object to be negated in establishing selflessness. (This includes anything considered to be) existent by way of its own characteristics, existent through its own entity, ultimately existent, truly existent, existent as (its own) reality, and so forth.

When meditating on selflessness, you must clearly identify how (the object of negation) is apprehended by your own innate misconception of self unalloyed with intellectually acquired conceptions. Detailed recognition of this comes about through cultivating close relations with a spiritual friend of the great vehicle and pleasing him for a long time. Therefore, such a method must be thoroughly pursued, just as the great being Haribhadra has said,

> The undistorted instruction is to please the spiritual friend impeccably.

HOW INNATE IGNORANCE, THE CONCEPTION OF 'I' AND 'MINE', ACTS AS THE ROOT OF CYCLIC EXISTENCE

When 'I' and 'mine' are apprehended as existing by way of their own characteristics, attachment to self arises within and that generates craving for all kinds of happiness for ourselves. The happiness of the 'I' is not found independently, without reliance on the happiness which is mine. As a consequence, craving for 'my happiness' prevents us from seeing its faults, so we only see its good qualities. As a result, the concept of 'mine' is accepted as a means for bringing about happiness for the 'I'. The disturbing emotions thus generated give rise to compositional action and that in turn propels us into birth in cyclic existence. Nāgārjuna's *Seventy Stanzas on Emptiness* says,

> Actions are caused by disturbing emotions,
> Karmic formations have a disturbed nature and
> The body is caused by karmic actions,
> So all three are empty of their own entity.

Train yourself until you have clearly ascertained this process of cyclic existence.

THE NEED TO DETERMINE SELFLESSNESS

The way to eliminate ignorance completely is as follows. We have to eliminate it by familiarising ourselves with the absence, established through reasoning, of the object of its mode of apprehension in relation to whatever object it focuses on. The great being Dharmakīrti has said (in his *Commentary on Dignāga's 'Compendium of Valid Cognition'*),

> Without discarding this object
> One is unable to eliminate it.

Instead of doing that, if we 1) merely familiarise ourselves with collecting and stabilising our thoughts; or 2) we acquaint ourselves with a nonconceptual state in which thoughts about whether things are existent or nonexistent, whether they are or are not, no longer arise; or 3) if, in meditation following analysis of the general appearance of what is negated, our analytical understanding differs from the meaning intended, or we meditate merely on a non-conceptual state in which we do not recognise (emptiness), however long we prolong the meditation we will never be able to rid ourselves of the seed of the misconception of self.

With regard to the first, even though the mind is not involved with the self to be negated, it does not actually apprehend the opposite of the way the misconception of self apprehends, because it is not involved with selflessness. The *Commentary on Dignāga's 'Compendium of Valid Cognition'* also states,

> Since love and so forth do not (directly) counter ignorance
> They cannot eliminate that grave fault.

The second (mistaken approach) is to confuse any and all the objects of any kind of conceptuality apprehending existence, nonexistence and so forth, with the object apprehended by the conception of true existence, that is to say, true existence which is the object of negation established by the reasoning that determines selflessness. This is like rekindling the system of the Chinese abbot, Hva Shang, for the object of negation is too extensive.

The third (mistaken approach) is to establish something other (than the view of selflessness) through analytical awareness, so that when we meditate our meditation is misplaced. Since it is unrelated (to the right view), it is like being shown the racetrack, yet running in the opposite direction. Moreover, since clinging onto any specific objective base is the basis for what is apprehended, we must discern the factor that counteracts the manner in which we apprehend it. To do otherwise is like trying to catch a thief, but avoiding following his tracks, or like making an appeasement offering at the western door to a spirit who has fled through the eastern door.

THE WAY TO DETERMINE THE VIEW OF SELFLESSNESS

This includes the order for establishing the two selflessnesses and actual techniques for establishing (the view of) selflessness.

THE ORDER FOR ESTABLISHING THE TWO SELFLESSNESSES

Firstly, as explained above, although there is not the slightest difference in subtlety regarding the self which does not exist in phenomena, whether the basis is the person or the mental and physical aggregates, because of a difference in subtlety in the basis of negation, there is a difference of ease in ascertaining (the view).

It is like this, in order for a person such as Devadatta to appear as an object to our minds we have to depend on apprehending his aggregates, so his imputed existence can be established through reason. Thus, there is not the slightest difference in subtlety with regard to what is negated in establishing the selflessness of phenomena, such as an image reflected in a mirror, a vase or a piece of cloth. However, because it is easier for some bases of negation to appear to our minds (such as our own persons compared to other phenomena), it is correspondingly easier or more difficult to ascertain selflessness. Also the *Condensed Perfection of Wisdom Sutra* says,

> Just as (you understand selflessness) in yourself,
> understand it similarly in all sentient beings.
> Just as (you understand selflessness) in all sentient beings, understand it similarly in all phenomena.

The actual techniques for establishing (the view of) selflessness have three aspects: how to determine the selflessness of persons, how to determine the selflessness of phenomena, and how, in dependence on this, persons and phenomena appear like illusions.

HOW TO DETERMINE THE SELFLESSNESS OF PERSONS

To begin with, this concerns recognition of what the basis, the person, is. All (Buddhists) agree that the focal object of the innate conception of an 'I' is the person. For some, such as followers of the Hearer tradition (the Particularists) the focal object of the (conception of the person) is the five mental and physical aggregates. For others, the person is only the mind. All Mind Only proponents of 'mere consciousness', who assert the existence of the 'mind basis of all' consciousness[54], take the 'mind basis of all' as the basis in relation to which the thought of 'I' arises when the disturbed mind focuses on it. Those proponents of 'mere consciousness' who do not assert the collection of the eight consciousnesses, and the followers of the master Bhāvaviveka (the Middle Way Inherence Validators), as well as the Sutra Followers, posit the sixth consciousness, the stream of mental consciousness, as the person. The master Bhāvaviveka established his assertion that the person is the mindstream, by means of both scripture and logic, in his *Blaze of Reasoning*.

All of them assert that the person is a mere imputation imputed to the mental and physical aggregates and that its representation must be something substantially existent. This is because when its existence is being posited by valid cognition and the imputed object is sought, it must be findable, for if it does not exist due to its own characteristics, it cannot exist at all.

Our own system comes from the words of the master Chandrakīrti, who in his *Supplement* thoroughly rejects (the premise) that the focal object of the innate conception of an 'I' is the aggregates. In his *Commentary* (to the *Supplement*) by saying that the imputed self is the focal object, he implies that, the thought of an 'I' must arise naturally in relation to it. And with regard to such things as the aggregates, the thought of 'mine' naturally arises, never the thought of 'I'. (Since we reject the aggregates as being the self, only the thought of 'mine' can arise in relation to them. The thought of 'I' cannot do so because it arises as an imputation in dependence on the aggregates.) This will become clear when we examine our own experience.

Every person, whether a man or woman, an exalted or ordinary individual, within cyclic existence or liberated from it, is designated in dependence upon the aggregates which form the basis of designation. In this regard, neither the continuity of the assembly of the aggregates, nor the assembly, nor the parts of the assembly, nor the continuity itself, nor even the one to whom that belongs, are the person. Take the example of a chariot: it is designated in dependence upon its various parts such as the wheels. None of its individual parts, nor the collection of the parts, is the chariot. Likewise, it is said in a sutra,

> Just as we speak of a chariot
> Dependent on the collection of parts,
> So we speak of a 'sentient being'
> Conventionally in dependence on its aggregates.

Such a technique for determining the selflessness of the person is one of the best methods for cognising the reality of things quickly. The same reasoning should be applied to all phenomena from form up to the omniscient mind. In order to determine in such a way that there is no inherently existent person, we establish that there is no inherently existent 'I', and then that there is no inherently existent 'mine'.

Firstly, when we generate the view of selflessness in our mental continuums, due to the faultless logical reasoning of being free from being (inherently) one or many the connected object (true existence) is not observed and through the reasoning of dependent arising the opposite (of true existence) is observed. Having examined our own continuums to begin with, the vital point is to recognise how the innate misconception of a self of persons conceives its object. This has already been explained.

OF THE TWO MEDITATIVE TECHNIQUES, ANALYTICAL AND FORMAL-ANALYSIS IS AS FOLLOWS

In determining (selflessness) by means of the (reasoning that things are) free from existing (truly) as one or distinct from (the basis of designation), were the person to exist inherently, it would have to exist invariably as one entity with the aggregates, or as a different entity. It definitely has no other mode of existence than these two. This is because, in general, whenever we prove that any phenomenon such as a vase has parts, the opposite, that it is partless, is refuted. (Likewise), when we validly establish that a single object is partless, the opposite, that it has parts, is refuted. As there is no way (for something to exist) apart from its being either the same as or different from (something else) we should be convinced that there is no other (mode of existence) than these two.

THE CONSEQUENCE OF THE SELF'S BEING ONE

There are three reasons stated to counteract the assertion that the person and aggregates are inherently one by way of their own characteristics. The first concerns the fallacies of asserting the self (as such).

If the self and aggregates were of one nature, existing by way of their own characteristics, the cognition to which they appeared as an object would be undistorted. This is because it would be a consciousness to which inherent existence appeared as an object. This would be similar to the (view of) the followers of the Hearer tradition (the Particularists), who assert that the sensory consciousness to which blue appears, which arises from a firm instinctive potency, is not distorted with regard to the object appearing to it.[55]

In this context, (if self and the aggregates are of one nature,) the final way in which the self and aggregates exist must be consistent with the way in which they appear to conceptual thought. In that case, they could not appear as two different things, because the way they appear to conceptuality and the way the two objects exist should be consistent and the objects' mode of existence is held to be of one nature in terms of inherent existence. If that were so these two would be one without the slightest distinction, and from that point of view even their appearing separately to thought would be impossible. Thus, since the aggregates are adopted (at birth) and discarded (at death), to assert such a self would be meaningless, because the self would be terminated, as being merely a portion of the aggregates. This is untenable. The *Fundamental Treatise Called 'Wisdom'* says,

> There is no self apart from that designated upon
> The contaminated aggregates. If, when they act as such,
> The contaminated aggregates themselves are the self,
> Your self will be nonexistent (after death).

THE CONSEQUENCE OF THE SELF'S BEING MANY

The second (fallacy, if the self and the aggregates are of one nature) is that there would consequently be many selves. If the self and aggregates were undifferentiably and indistinguishably one, since everyone has many aggregates, the person would have many selves. Otherwise, because the person is singular and inseparably one (with the aggregates), the aggregates would become one. This is unacceptable. Chandrakīrti's *Supplement* says,

> If the aggregates are the self, since they are numerous
> It follows that there will also be many selves.

THE CONSEQUENCE OF THE SELF'S BEING CREATED AND DESTROYED

The third (fallacy, if the self and the aggregates are of one nature) reveals the consequences of the self's being created and destroyed. Just as the aggregates, which are asserted to be the same as the person, are created (at birth) and destroyed (at death), so too would the person have to be created and destroyed. When what is created and destroyed exists inherently, (the person and aggregates) could not be anything other than of the same or different natures, and yet both of these would be unacceptable. So, if they were inherently the same, each established by way of its own characteristics, it would be as if the person of this and the previous life were the same without distinction. If that were the case and you and the continuity (of your previous life) were the same, a person would have been born in this life without having died, because he would be inseparably one with the person (you are) in this life. It is unreasonable to make such statements because (the person) would then be permanent. *The Fundamental Treatise Called 'Wisdom'* says,

> If that god were (born as) this man,
> Such (a person) would be permanent.

If persons linked together by former and later lives were of a different nature, existing by way of their own characteristics, it would be impossible for there to be any connection between them. There would be no relationship (in terms of the causes and results of actions) between each self, because they would both be of a different nature. Their arising would be unconnected, because their both (being inherently different) would contradict the dependence of one thing upon another. As the inherent existence of one thing contradicts its being related to something else, it is inappropriate to posit a relationship between them, because they share neither of the two relations (cause and effect or being of the same entity). (If persons were to exist inherently, they would have not to depend on anything else, but if something has a relationship with anything else it must also depend on something else.) The *Supplement* says,

> Whatever exists individually, by way of its own characteristics,
> Cannot possibly belong to one continuity.

If persons were not of the same continuity, recollection of past lives would be unacceptable. If such were the case, it would contradict many sutras (in which the Buddha recalled his previous lives as a Bodhisattva on the spiritual path. Even our own recollection of previous actions would be impossible, if the self of today were inherently different from that of yesterday.) Moreover, the wholesome and unwholesome actions that someone has done in his previous life would be dissipated and he would not experience their outcome. This is because we cannot assert that his (actions) will be experienced by another person who is of the same continuity as himself. This would be like saying that a person meets in this life with the happy and miserable results of prior actions, without having done them. Because we cannot assert that they were accumulated by another person of the same continuity as himself, it would follow that he had never accumulated their causes.

Thus, having sought through the path of logical reasoning to ascertain the fallacies of the person and the aggregates existing by way of their own characteristics while being of the same nature, we should maintain this understanding.

According to our own tradition, we must accept that the

person and the aggregates are nominally of the same entity, which is an extremely subtle and difficult point. If the person and aggregates, existing by way of their own characteristics, were of a different nature, as the *Fundamental Treatise Called 'Wisdom'* says,

> If (the self) is different from the aggregates,
> The aggregates will have no characteristics.

The aggregates would then lack the three characteristics of creation, abidance and destruction, which make them composite phenomena. They would be like a horse and an ox, which being of different entities, do not share each other's characteristics. If it were so (that the aggregates and the person existed inherently) it would not be possible for them to form a composite phenomenon. In that case, they would not be an object of either the mode of apprehension, or its aspect, of the innate misconception of a self of persons, like, for example, space and the state beyond sorrow.

Moreover, if the person and the aggregates are of different entities in terms of existing by way of their own characteristics, even if there were no aggregates at all as a basis, an uncontrived thought of an 'I' should arise without them. For instance, a vase's being of a different entity from a piece of cloth (means that) even when there is no vase as a basis, we can produce the thought that this is a piece of cloth and on the other hand, if there were no cloth as a basis, we would still be able to generate the thought that this is a vase, without making it up. The *Fundamental Treatise Called 'Wisdom'* says,

> It is not at all acceptable for the self
> To be other than the contaminated aggregates,
> For without the contaminated aggregates, even if you
> Think there's something to be apprehended, there isn't.

And the *Supplement* says,

> Therefore, there is no self apart from the aggregates

> Because that self cannot be conceived without depending on the aggregates.

(Thus, the person does not exist by way of its own characteristics, because it depends on the aggregates.)

Accordingly, when you have properly seen the invalidity of the person and aggregates being one or different in nature, by way of their own characteristics, they are established as neither inherently one nor different. Through the reasoning which negates the pervasion (of inherent existence), once the pervasive factor (of being inherently one or many) has been negated, valid cognition properly ascertaining the lack of inherent existence of the person. This ascertainment should be nurtured through mindfulness and alertness.

THE TECHNIQUE FOR DETERMINING THE LACK OF AN INHERENTLY EXISTENT 'MINE'

Once we have validly ascertained that the self (of the person) has no inherent existence for the reason that it is neither one nor many, relying on the force of that very reason, we shall come to realise that 'mine' also is devoid of inherent existence. For having validly understood that a barren woman has no son, we need go no further in order to understand that he does not have a pale or a radiant complexion. The *Fundamental Treatise Called 'Wisdom'* says,

> If the self does not exist
> How will 'mine' exist?

and the *Supplement* says,

> Because the agent does not exist (inherently) his actions do not exist.
> Therefore, 'mine' has no self-existence.
> Thus, the yogi who (meditates on) the view that 'self' and 'mine'

> Are empty of (inherent existence) will be released
> (from cyclic existence).

We should familiarise ourselves accordingly with the understanding that all persons, exalted and ordinary beings, who are of a different continuum from ourselves, lack an (inherently existent) self. The *Condensed Perfection of Wisdom Sutra* says,

> Just as the self (is empty of inherent existence) understand
> every sentient being similarly,
> Just as every sentient being (is empty of inherent existence)
> understand all phenomena similarly.

(This concludes the explanation of the methods for ascertaining the selflessness of the person involving the four points of analysis according to the view of the great Nāgārjuna.)

How to Determine the Selflessness of Phenomena

The techniques for determining the selflessness of phenomena involve taking the mental and physical aggregates, the spheres of sensory cognition and the bases of the cognitive faculties as indicative of phenomena.

It is extremely important to recognise that the object to be negated, which in this case is what is apprehended by the innate conception of true existence projected onto those (phenomena), is neither too extensive nor too narrow. The ways in which we misconceive (things as truly existent) have already been explained.

The way to determine selflessness by means of the (reasoning) that phenomena, such as the aggregates, are free from truly being one or many, is to discard the notion that existence as we understand it is partless. When we have established through reasoning that an existent phenomenon has parts, and analyzed that the parts and the possessor of parts (for instance the body and its limbs) are naturally of the same or different natures in terms of existing by way of their own characteristics, then for them to be inherently of one nature means they will exist as one, without any distinction whatsoever. If they are different in nature, we must reject any relationship between them (such as that between the aggregates and the person).

These methods (for determining) the lack of inherent existence, by establishing that things can exist neither as inherently the same nor as inherently different, are like those presented in the course of explaining the selflessness of persons. They should be understood by replacing the subject or phenomenon accordingly.

The manner in which the lack of inherent existence is determined by employing the reason of the existence of the opposite (of inherent existence—dependent arising) is as follows.

It is easy to ascertain that all relationships, internal and external, such as those between the mental and physical aggregates, arise in dependence (upon something else). The way to refute a common basis between such relationships and inherent existence is as follows: it is contradictory for anything to exist inherently and be in contact with something else, and whatever exists in dependence (on causes and conditions) must be in contact with something else. For instance, a reflection in a mirror must arise in dependence on many causes and conditions (such as the mirror's being clean, the position of the reflected object, the perceiver and so forth). If it is its nature to be able to stand under its own power, it must appear undistortedly to the perceiving mind to which it appears. And if that is so, the way in which it appears there and the reflection's actual mode of subsistence should be consistent. Because inconsistency is proved by reality, we see that finding a common basis between inherent existence and dependent arising, based on (the example of) a reflection, is contradictory. (The reflection of a face in a mirror appears to be a face. For this appearance to comply with the actual mode of subsistence, the reflection should be a face in the mirror. Because it is not, the perception is distorted with regard to the object that appears to it.)

When you have realised that dependent arising is empty of inherent existence, apply (your understanding) to all phenomena. There is scope for two kinds of mistake in realising the pure view of selflessness, the views of eternalism and nihilism. When all internal and external phenomena are validly established as dependent arisings, all nihilistic views will be driven far away. When the meaning of the assertion of the lack of inherent existence is validly established, through seeing the contradiction of not finding a common factor between dependent arising and inherent existence, all eternalistic views will be left far behind.

In praise of dependent arising, the king of reasoning, the *Questions of Anavatapta, King of the Nāgas, Sūtra* says,

> Anything produced from conditions lacks production,
> For it is not born from its own entity.
> Whatever depends on conditions is explained as empty,
> Whoever understands emptiness is at ease.

Also the *Supplement* says,

> By virtue of (the reasoning that) things arise in dependence
> upon each other
> It is impossible to impute such conceptions (of production
> from self, other and so forth).
> Therefore, by using the reasoning of dependent arising
> The net of all wrong views is severed.

These techniques for meditation on the selflessness of persons and phenomena through reasoned analysis have been explained in brief. This very emptiness, which is a lack of inherent existence of persons or phenomena, pervades everything from form to the omniscient mind. It is not as if it were something merely occasional, for emptiness is totally pervasive.

Moreover, it is not as if we search with reasoning for something that was not naturally empty before and arrive at emptiness. This would be an emptiness contrived by the intellect, yet it is not so. Emptiness has been present from the very beginning. Having established emptiness in such a way, it is not as though it is the emptiness of the nihilists, who do not know how to establish the validity of action and agent, for emptiness is always pre-eminent. Nor is it as if emptiness is something beyond perception, that we cannot be aware of, understand or cognise. Nor is realising and impressing emptiness on our minds without significance, for in cognising and comprehending it we are released from the two obstructions, together with their instinctive propensities, and are admitted to the ranks of liberation and omniscience. Thus, (realisation of emptiness) is the sole path along which (the Hearers, Solitary Realisers and Bodhisattvas) of the three vehicles proceed.

TECHNIQUES FOR MAINTAINING (THE VIEW) IN FORMAL MEDITATION

As was explained above, when our minds are distracted towards the self to be negated it is not appropriate merely to withdraw them. Nor should we meditate on nothing but a nonconceptual state in which we do not adhere to any such notions as 'existent' or 'nonexistent', 'is' or 'is not'. Nor, once we have found by reasoned examination that there is no inherent existence, should we meditate on something other than that.

With regard to the way in which all four theses stated by Nāgārjuna, when he says, not (produced) from self, (other, both, and neither), are exclusively nonaffirming negations, all the great pioneers, (Indian masters such as Āryadeva, Buddhapālita, Chandrakīrti, Shāntideva, Shāntarakṣhīta, and Atīsha) unanimously concur in word and thought.

In maintaining the view of selflessness, once we have properly ascertained the mode of apprehension of the innate misconception of self, whatever object it apprehends and in whatever way it apprehends it, the vital point is to maintain the (view of) nonaffirmation, as a result of having negated the mode of apprehension of the object the way it apprehends it and not otherwise.

Furthermore, in explaining the techniques for meditating on the selflessness of persons, the object of the mode of apprehension of the innate misconception of self, which is projected onto the mere 'I', is (the self's having) inherent existence, or existing by way of its own characteristics, or existing due to its own entity and so forth. Therefore, we should value and never be separated from the ascertainment of the view, the lack of inherent existence of the basis, the person.

For some people, to say, 'there is no inherent I', is no more than empty words, and they say we should maintain that, 'the 'I' does not have that (nature)', 'the 'I' does not exist in that way', and 'the 'I' does not exist in the way it appears'. When we examine these statements and maintain that the basis 'I' does not have the nature (of true existence), having allowed the generic image of the object of negation, as described above, to appear properly in relation to the basis 'I', there is no scope for thinking of such statements as mere empty words. If we do not recognise the generic image of the object of negation properly after allowing it to appear, how could such statements not be empty words?

Therefore, the definitive object relating to the view, which all the scriptures take as a literal expression teaching the profound (subject of emptiness), must be asserted to be: the (actual) nature of that which acts as a basis; reality; the mode of subsistence; the ultimate truth, and so on.

TECHNIQUES FOR ACTUALISING A CALMLY ABIDING MIND THAT APPREHENDS THE SELFLESSNESS OF PERSONS OR PHENOMENA

It is essential to have assembled the factors for a calmly abiding mind so that, when selflessness is the object on which the mind is focused, the meditative absorption that is to be actualised is clear and nonconceptual. When it is hindered by laxity and excitement, employ mindfulness as an antidote. Recognising even their subtle aspects by means of introspection, persist in your meditation in such a way that you do not come under their influence.

The order of the (nine) stages of setting the mind is as follows: setting the mind on the object, continual setting, patchlike setting, close setting, controlling, pacifying, total pacification, making single-pointed, and the stage of equilibrium.

The technique for actualising these through the six forces and the four activities is as follows. On the first stage employ the force of listening (to the instructions) and on the second, the force of thinking about them. On the next two stages employ the force of mindfulness (to keep the mind on the object). On the two stages after that the force of introspection (counters subtle laxity and subtle excitement). On the two following stages employ vigour and on the ninth stage apply the force of thorough familiarity.

The way the four mental activities are (engaged is as follows). On the first two stages is the mental activity of deliberate engagement. During the following five stages there is the mental activity of interrupted engagement and on the eighth stage that of uninterrupted engagement. On the ninth stage is the mental activity of spontaneous engagement, due to familiarity with which there is no need for further exertion.

Then, having gently relaxed your effort with regard to laxity and excitement in relation to the actual object, when familiarity (with the practice) yields extreme physical and mental pliancy, a calmly abiding mind has been attained. (Maitreya's *Discrimination Between the Middle Way and the Extremes* says,)

> Then such a body and mind,
> Having gained great pliancy,
> Must be engaged and put to use.

Having actualised a calmly abiding mind in this way, examine the significance of selflessness as before. Then, having gained familiarity with the technique for balancing a calmly abiding mind and discriminating awareness, when you are able to derive fresh pliancy from the impact of analytical meditation itself, not merely the previous pliancy, that is the gauge of having actualised special insight.

A calmly abiding mind and special insight (should) be interrelated or possess common features, (such as a common object, relying on the same sensory base, arising simultaneously, having the same aspect and a common entity). The sage Shāntipa has said,

> If you possess the methods, as explained, for mutually binding a calmly abiding mind and special insight, one to the other, they will give rise to the meditation on special insight apprehending emptiness.

HOW PERSONS AND PHENOMENA APPEAR LIKE ILLUSIONS

Once we have understood both analytical and formal meditation in this way, there is a technique for taking the practice to heart in the post-meditational period. (As the text says,)

In the period between sessions be a creator of illusions

In general, the mere notion of 'illusions' is accepted by everyone, Buddhists and outsiders, but there are two ways to take the analogy of illusions, that (things) appear like illusions, or that they really are (illusions).

THE ARTIFICIAL WAY IN WHICH THINGS APPEAR LIKE ILLUSIONS

Some people, not inclined towards understanding things as they are, when searching for the way in which things exist, maintain (a state) of mere nonconceptuality. When they rise (from meditation) appearances emerge indistinctly. Moreover, at such times the substantial, solid, impenetrable appearance of mountains, buildings, houses and so forth vanishes, and they appear translucent like smoke or the colours of a rainbow. Appearances like these are not what is meant by illusions, for things to appear as illusory in this context, there must first be a refutation of (true existence) by analytical awareness with respect to the basis.

The way some earlier scholars explained persons and phenomena as being like illusions was, to use the (common) analogy, to assert that just as the pebbles and sticks (that the conjurer uses as the basis of his illusion) appear as horses and elephants, yet are empty of being horses and elephants, so although men, women and so on appear to be persons, they are empty of being persons. And although the mental and physical aggregates, the spheres of sensory cognition, the bases of the cognitive faculties and so forth appear to be as they are, they are empty of being such things. Similarly, (they asserted) that everything is like a dream, a mirage and so on.

These interpretations should be questioned. What does it mean to say that men, women and so on are empty of being themselves? If they were not themselves, these phenomena would be totally nonexistent. If they do exist, (they) must exist as themselves, since (otherwise) they would not exist as what they are. In such cases, (these scholars) have not properly gauged the extent of what is to be negated and, from relying on an insufficient image (of what is to be negated), they maintain a perverted interpretation of the scriptures, which teach about illusions, dreams and so forth, merely employing jargon associated with the common word 'selflessness'.

Given the system of negating the object to be negated, if the extent of what is to be negated is not properly assessed, it will be impossible validly to establish the basis. At such points, having become familiar with the significance of not finding any basis whatsoever, such as (the basis of) the analyser, the process of analysis and so forth, the arising of blurred appearances of these things is not the meaning of an illusion. That being the case, it is completely wrong to generate a view that underestimates appearances while cognising the lack of true existence.

THE PERFECT WAY IN WHICH THINGS APPEAR AS ILLUSIONS

The King of Meditative Stabilisations Sutra says,

> Just like a mirage and the city of the Gandharvas [56],
> Similar to an illusion and just like a dream,
> Contemplating these signs of being empty of reality,
> Understand all phenomena in the same way.

The *Perfection of Wisdom Sūtra* says,

> For instance, when it is said that ultimate truth is illusory, this is interpreted (as meaning) that (they are like illusions in that) although things exist their true (existence) is negated, and (there is) the interpretation that while things are empty they appear and that appearance is like an illusion. Of these two it is the latter.

I will explain this in a way that is easier to understand. When the magician conjures up a horse or elephant from a pebble or stick, the appearance of the horse or elephant is established by direct valid perception (of the visual consciousness), while mental consciousness ascertains that it is empty of existing in the way it appears. Combining these two aspects like this is how things appear like illusions.

Ordinary persons and exalted beings, and all phenomena, such as the aggregates, actions, that which is acted upon, the agent and so forth are correctly established by a nominally valid (cognition). The subtle object of negation, which, as explained above, is projected onto these bases, is eradicated by analytical awareness. When these two factors are brought together, (things) appear as illusions. Moreover, once we have carried out the space-like equipoise on emptiness and gone to the very heart of the practice, when we arise from it and the appearance of objects is illusory, there is no need to seek further techniques.

When initially meditating on emptiness, through mixing

the basis of negation (such as a person) and that which is to be negated (the person's inherent existence) together as one, they cannot appear individually, therefore their illusory appearance is weak. But, as explained above, through faultlessly cognising the meaning of emptiness and gaining familiarity with it over a long period of time by not relinquishing the factors and conditions of meditation, your intellect will reach the limit of perfection.

The great Bodhisattva Che-ka-wa's advice on training in the precious awakening mind, the excellent whispered lineage of the great vehicle mind training known as the Rays of the Sun has been explained according to the whispered instructions of the venerable master who has mastery over the ocean-like teachings of the Ones Thus Gone, the sublime navigator, the great King of the Doctrine, Tsong-kha-pa. The final view concerning the subtlest essence of these subjects should be discerned from this venerated teacher's *Great Exposition of the Stages of the Path to Enlightenment.*

This process of acquainting yourself with the awakening mind
Is the uncommon cause for actualising a Buddha's wisdom;
Is the only entrance for venturing into the great vehicle;
Is like a fire burning off the thicket of faulty actions;
And is a treasury of jewels providing all prosperity.
The supreme being, the Powerful Subduer, who speaks about (the vast and profound doctrine),
The chief of his sons, invincible Maitreya and refined, glorious and eloquent Mañjushri,
Nāgārjuna and Asaṅga who opened up the tradition for the carriers of the teaching to pass through,
Shāntideva and glorious Atīsha, who have generated the altruistic mind,
And transmitted it from ear to ear,
Showered their teachings on the Bodhisattva Che-ka-wa,
Who created these techniques for (engendering) the precious awakening mind.

The way to generate it in your continuum is through the four preliminary practices
And the process of training in the twofold awakening mind, which is the actual basis.
You should clearly distinguish between the common and the uncommon
Systems of each of the great pioneers of the teachings,
Especially that supreme tradition of Shāntiḍeva
Of training in the awakening mind through the exchange of self with others
And that of Che-ka-wa, a Conqueror's Son, so that in integrating
These two trainings of the mind into the total body of the path
You will have the technique for practising the subtlest attributes of the teaching.
I have clearly explained everything in such a way.
Whatever has been elucidated in accordance with the unsurpassable Doctrine
In these words of advice, is due to the kindness of my teachers.
It is difficult to fathom the intention of the Conquerors and their sons
And I am one of inferior intellect and small exertion,
So if, in collecting these explanations together, I have failed to explain them correctly,
I declare such faults from my heart before those having the eye of the Doctrine.
By the force of whatever accumulation of wholesome virtue
I have amassed from this endeavour,
May I and every living being throughout all space
Never be parted from the awakening mind.
May the force of that dispel every trace of misery
And bestow happiness and benefit on wandering beings throughout the three realms
Through their body, speech and mind seeing, hearing, recollecting and making contact (with the Doctrine)
For as long as cyclic existence remains.

THE TIBETAN PUBLISHER'S COLOPHON

This explanation of the superb whispered transmission of the great vehicle mind training entitled the *Rays of the Sun* has been composed by Nam-kha Pel, who faced persistent requests from people with great faith in these teachings. Having cultivated his thoughts and actions for twelve years in accordance with the most wonderful King of the Doctrine, Tsong-kha-pa, he is a repository of many discourses on sutra and mantra, and dwells in the blessings of many realised beings. He composed it while residing in solitude at Rin-chen Ling Monastery.

Part Three
APPENDICES

THE SEVEN POINT MIND TRAINING

Thog-me Zang-po's Edition

Homage to great compassion.

First, train in the preliminaries.

Consider all phenomena as like dreams,
Examine the nature of unborn awareness.
The remedy itself is released in its own place,
Set the entity of the path on the nature of the basis of all.
In the period between sessions be a creator of illusions.

Practise a combination of giving and taking,
These two should be made to ride on the breath.
Concerning the three objects, three poisons and the three virtues,
Be mindful of the practice in general
By taking these words to heart in all activities.
You should begin acceptance with yourself.

When the environment and its inhabitants overflow with unwholesomeness,
Transform adverse circumstances into the path to enlightenment.

Banish the one to blame for everything,
Meditate on the great kindness of all beings.

To see confusion as the four bodies
The protection of emptiness is unsurpassable.

The supreme method is accompanied by the four practices,
Apply meditation immediately at every opportunity.

In brief, the essence of the instructions
Is to train in the five powers.

The five powers themselves are the great vehicle's
Precept on the transference of consciousness,
Cultivate these paths of practice.

Integrate all the teachings into one thought;
Primary importance should be given to the two witnesses.
Constantly cultivate only a peaceful mind,
The trained (mind) retains control even when distracted.

Always train in the three general points.
Transform your intention but maintain your natural behaviour,
Don't speak of others' incomplete qualities,
Don't concern yourself with others' business,
Deal with the stronger disturbing emotions first,
Give up every hope of reward,
Avoid poisonous food,
Don't maintain inverted loyalty,
Don't make malicious banter,
Don't lie in ambush,
Don't strike at the vital point,
Don't place the load of a horse on a pony,
Don't sprint to win the race,
Don't be treacherous,
Do not turn gods into devils,
Don't seek others' misery as a means to happiness.

Every yoga should be performed as one,
All errors are to be amended by one means.
There are two activities at both beginning and end.
Whichever occurs be patient with both.
Guard both at the cost of your life.

Train in the three difficulties,
Seek for the three principal causes,
Don't let three factors weaken,
Never be parted from the three possessions,
Train consistently without partiality,
Don't apply a wrong understanding,
Don't be sporadic,
Practise unflinchingly,
Release investigation and analysis,
Don't be boastful,
Don't be short-tempered,
Don't make a short-lived attempt,
Don't expect gratitude.

This time of the five degenerations is then transformed
Into the path to the fully awakened state.
The essence of this nectar of secret instruction
Is transmitted from the master from Sumatra.
Due to the awakening of the seeds of previous actions
My manifold aspirations have given rise
To humiliating criticisms and sufferings,
But, having received instructions for taming the misconception of self,
Even if I die I have no regrets.

THE SEVEN POINT MIND TRAINING

Pha-bong-kha Rin-po-che's Edition

Homage to great compassion.
The essence of this nectar of secret instruction
Is transmitted from the master from Sumatra.

REVEALING THE FEATURES OF THE DOCTRINE TO ENGENDER RESPECT FOR THE INSTRUCTION

You should understand the significance of this instruction
As like a diamond, the sun and a medicinal tree.
This time of the five degenerations will then be transformed
Into the path to the fully awakened state.

THE ACTUAL INSTRUCTION FOR GUIDING THE DISCIPLE IS GIVEN IN SEVEN POINTS

1. *Explaining the preliminaries as a basis for the practice*

First, train in the preliminaries.

2. *The actual practice, training in the awakening mind*
   a. *How to train in the ultimate awakening mind*
   b. *How to train in the conventional awakening mind*

(According to most of the older records, the training in the ultimate awakening mind is dealt with first. However, according to our own tradition, following the gentle protector Tsong-kha-pa, as contained in such works as the *Mind Training Like the Rays of the Sun, Ornament for Lobsang's Thought, Essence of Nectar,* and Ke'utsang's *Root Words,* the order is reversed for special reasons.)

a. Training in the conventional awakening mind

Banish the one to blame for everything,
Meditate on the great kindness of all beings,
Practise a combination of giving and taking.
Giving and taking should be practised alternately
And you should begin by taking from yourself.
These two should be made to ride on the breath

Concerning the three objects, three poisons, and three virtues,
The instruction to be followed, in short,
Is to be mindful of the practice in general,
By taking these words to heart in all activities.

b. Training in the ultimate awakening mind

When stability has been attained, impart the secret teaching:
Consider all phenomena as like dreams,
Examine the nature of unborn awareness.
The remedy itself is released in its own place,
Place the essence of the path on the nature of the basis of all.

In the period between sessions be a creator of illusions.

3. Transforming adverse circumstances into the path to enlightenment

When the environment and its inhabitants overflow with unwholesomeness,
Transform adverse circumstances into the path to enlightenment.
Apply meditation immediately at every opportunity.
The supreme method is accompanied by the four practices.

4. The integrated practice of a single lifetime

In brief, the essence of the instruction is
To train in the five powers.
The five powers themselves are the great vehicle's
Precept on the transference of consciousness.
Cultivate these paths of practice.

5. The measure of having trained the mind

Integrate all the teachings into one thought,
Primary importance should be given to the two witnesses,
Constantly cultivate only a peaceful mind.
The measure of a trained mind is that it has turned away,
There are five great marks of a trained mind.
The trained (mind) retains control even when distracted.

6. The commitments of mind training

1. Don't go against the mind training you promised to observe,
2. Don't be reckless in your practice,
3. Don't be partial, always train in the three general points,
4. Transform your attitude but maintain your natural behaviour,
5. Don't speak of others' incomplete qualities,
6. Don't concern yourself with others' business,
7. Train to counter whichever disturbing emotion is greatest,
8. Give up every hope of reward,
9. Avoid poisonous food,
10. Don't maintain misplaced loyalty,
11. Don't make sarcastic remarks
12. Don't lie in ambush,
13. Don't strike at the vital point,
14. Don't place the load of a horse on a pony,
15. Don't abuse the practice,

16 Don't sprint to win the race,
17 Don't turn gods into devils,
18 Don't seek others' misery as a means to happiness.

7. The precepts of mind training

1 Every yoga should be performed as one,
2 All errors are to amended by one means,
3 There are two activities at both beginning and end,
4 Whichever occurs be patient with both,
5 Guard both at the cost of your life,
6 Train in the three difficulties,
7 Seek for the three principal causes,
8 Don't let three factors weaken,
9 Never be parted from the three possessions,
10 Train consistently without partiality,
11 Value an encompassing and far-reaching practice,
12 Train consistently to deal with difficult situations,[1]
13 Don't rely on other conditions,
14 Engage in the principal practices right now,
15 Don't apply a wrong understanding,
16 Don't be sporadic,
17 Practise unflinchingly,
18 Release investigation and analysis,
19 Don't be boastful,
20 Don't be short-tempered,
21 Don't make a short-lived attempt,
22 Don't expect gratitude.

This is concluded with a quotation from Geshey Che-ka-wa, who had experience of the awakening mind:

My manifold aspirations have given rise
To humiliating criticism and suffering,

1 Regarding members of your family, enemies and rivals, those who harm you despite your helping them, and those you dislike on sight due to the influence of past actions.

But, having received instructions for taming the misconception of self,
Even if I have to die, I have no regrets.

(In the literature of the old and new Kadampa there are many versions of the commentaries and root text of the *Seven Point Mind Training*. The order of presentation and the number of words in them differs greatly. Some of them we cannot confidently incorporate within the outlines when we are giving an explanation, and some include unfamiliar verses in the root text. For these reasons I had been thinking for a long time of producing a definitive root text by collating the editions to be found in *Mind Training Like the Rays of the Sun*, *Ornament for Lobsang's Thought*, and *Essence of Nectar*. When I was teaching the *Stages of the Path to Enlightenment* at Chamdo Jampa-ling in 1935 (Wood Pig year), Lam-rim-pa Phuntsok Palden, a single-minded practitioner presented me a scarf and an offering and made such a request, so I have compiled this after careful research of many root texts and commentaries and supplemented it with outlines.)

OUTLINE OF THE MIND TRAINING LIKE THE RAYS OF THE SUN

The Author's Homage and Request
A Prayer of Devotion

I. INTRODUCTION
A. The Historical Account of the Teaching
B. The Unique Features, Value and Extraordinary Function of this Secret Instruction

II. EXPLANATION OF THE TEACHING
A. Contemplation of the Preliminary Teachings
- 1. Life as a Free and Fortunate Human Being
  - a. Contemplation of the rarity of such a human life according to the difficulty of obtaining the cause
  - b. Contemplation of the rarity of finding such a human life according to the difficulty of obtaining the result
- 2. How to Think About the Brevity of This Life, Death and Impermanence.
  - a. The inevitability of death
  - b. The uncertainty of the time of death
  - c. Only the doctrine can help at the time of death
- 3. Actions and Their Consequences
  - a. The certainty of actions and their results
  - b. The multiplying nature of actions
  - c. Not having to face the consequences of actions you have not done
  - d. Once committed actions do not fade away
- 4. The Drawbacks of Cyclic Existence
  - a. The disadvantages of uncertainty
  - b. The disadvantages of dissatisfaction
  - c. The disadvantages of having to discard your body over and over again
  - d. The disadvantages of entering the womb over and over again
  - e. The disadvantages of continually changing from high to low
  - f. The disadvantages of having no companions

B. The Steps for Actually Training in the Precious Awakening Mind, the Actual Basis of the Practice
- 1. Cultivating the Conventional Awakening Mind
  - a. Appreciating the Value of the Awakening Mind, the entrance to the great vehicle

- b. Actual Techniques for Cultivating the Awakening Mind
  - (1) Instructions for Actually Training in the Conventional Awakening Mind
    - (a) The Process of Cultivating the Awakening Mind That is Concerned with the Welfare of Others
      - i) Exchanging yourself with others through acknowledging the faults of selfishness and the advantages of concern for others
        - a) What is to be given up by contemplating the advantages of selfishness
        - b) What is to be put into practice through contemplating the advantages of concern for others
      - ii) Actually Cultivating the Awakening Mind that is Concerned with the Interests of Others
        - a) Taking the practice to heart in the context of an actual meditation session
          - (i) Meditation on Love
            - a') How to dispense your body, possessions and virtues in general
              - i') Giving to the inhabitants (who are living beings)
                - a") Giving to those not engaged in the spiritual path
                  - i") Giving in particular to those who harm us
                - b") Offering to those who are engaged in the spiritual path
              - ii') Giving to the environment (which beings inhabit)
            - b') Giving away possessions
            - c') Giving away virtues
          - (ii) Meditation on Compassion
            - a') Taking (sufferings) from the inhabitants, (living beings)
            - b') Taking (unsatisfactoriness) from the environment (which beings inhabit)
        - b) The practice to be followed in the periods after and in between meditation sessions
    - (b) The Process of Cultivating the Awakened Mind Concerned with Attaining the Fully Awakened State of Being
  - (2) Instructions Concerning the Five Precepts that are Factors of the Training

- (a) Transforming Adverse Circumstances into the Path
  - i) Brief explanation
  - ii) Elaborate explanation
    - a) Taking adverse circumstances into the path by relying on the special thought of the awakening mind
    - b) Taking adverse circumstances into the path by relying on the excellent practices of accumulation and purification
      - (i) Accumulation of merit
      - (ii) Purification of negativity
      - (iii) Making offerings to evil spirits
      - (iv) Offering ritual cakes to religious protectors and seeking their help
- (b) The Integrated Practice of a Single Lifetime
  - i) The power of intention
  - ii) The power of the white seed
  - iii) The power of remorse
  - iv) The power of prayer
  - v) The power of acquaintance
    - a) Applying the five powers at the time of death
      - (i) The power of the white seed
      - (ii) The power of intention
      - (iii) The power of remorse
      - (iv) The power of prayer
      - (v) The power of acquaintance
- (c) The Measure of Having Trained the Mind
  - i) Signs of a trained mind
- (d) The Irreversible Commitments of Mind Training
  - i) Explanation of what appears in the text in verse
    - a) Three general points of training
      - (i) Mind training that is not contrary to the commitments
      - (ii) Mind training which is not led astray
      - (iii) Mind training which is impartial
    - b) Five kinds of difficult situation
  - ii) Explanation of what appears in the text as maxims
- (e) The Precepts of Mind Training
  - i) Explanation of what appears in the text in verse
  - ii) Explanation of what appears in the text as maxims

2. Cultivating the Ultimate Awakening Mind
   - a. The type of person to whom the instructions should be given
   - b. The time for imparting the teachings.
   - c. The actual instructions on cultivating the ultimate awakening mind
     - (1) Recognising What Ignorance Is and How It Is the Source of Cyclic Existence

- (a) Recognising What Ignorance Is
- (b) How Innate Ignorance, the Conception of 'I' and 'Mine', Acts as the Source of Cyclic Existence

(2) In Order to Eradicate (Ignorance) We Need to Determine the View of Selflessness and also Have a Technique for Doing So
- (a) The Need to Determine Selflessness[57]
- (b) The Way to Determine the View of Selflessness
  - i) The order for establishing the two selflessnesses
  - ii) Actual techniques for establishing (the view of) selflessness
    - a) How to determine the selflessness of persons
      - (i) Of the two meditative techniques, analytical and formal analysis[58]
        - a') The consequence of the self's being one[59]
        - b') The consequence of the self's being many
        - c') The consequence of the self's being created and destroyed
      - (ii) The technique for determining the lack of an inherently existent 'mine'
    - b) How to determine the selflessness of phenomena
      - (i) Techniques for maintaining (the view) in formal meditation[60]
      - (ii) Techniques for actualising a calmly abiding mind that apprehends the selflessness of persons or phenomena
    - c) How persons and phenomena appear like illusions
      - (i) The artificial way in which things appear like illusions
      - (ii) The perfect way in which things appear as illusions.

NOTES

1. 'Brom-ston-pa
2. Po-to-ba, Phu-chung-ba, sPyan-snga-ba.
3. The awakening mind (*bodhichitta; byang chub sems*) in general is the altruistic aspiration to gain enlightenment for the sake of all sentient beings. It is the attitude which primarily distinguishes a Bodhisattva.
4. In Tibetan the expression translated here as 'misconception of self', *bdag 'dzin*, may be more literally rendered as 'conception of self'. However, in Tibetan this 'conception of self' is implicitly understood to indicate a misconception about the self. As virtually all Tibetan Buddhist traditions adhere to the Middle Way Consequentialist (*Prāsangika Mādhyamaka*) view, we can define this misconception about the self as seeing the self of persons or phenomena as inherently existent, existent due to its own characteristics and so forth.
5. Arhats are those who have actually attained the state beyond sorrow, nirvana, having overcome their disturbing emotions.
6. rGyal-ba'i-'byung-gnas
7. Urgyan, commonly thought to be situated in what is now N.W. Pakistan, is a mythical land whose inhabitants are believed to be tantric yogis.
8. Ra-treng (rva-phreng), was the site of the monastery founded by Drom-tön-pa.
9. Geshey (*kalyanamitra; bge ba'i bshes gnyen*) literally means spiritual or virtuous friend and was originally applied to accomplished teachers and practitioners of the Kadampa tradition founded by Atīsha and Drom-tön-pa. Only later did it come to have the connotation of an academic degree.
10. The Six Original Scriptures: *Ornament for Great Vehicle Sutras, (Mahāyanasūtralaṃkārakārikā; Theg pa chen po'i mdo sde'i rgyan gyi tshig le'ur byas pa)* by Asaṅga/Maitreya; *Spiritual Stages of Bodhisattva, (Yogacharyābhumau Bodhisattvabhūmi; rNal-'byor spyod-pa'i sa-las byang-chub sems-dpa'i-sa)* by Asaṅga; *Birth Stories,(Jātakamālā; sKyes pa'i rabs kyi rgyud)* by Āryashūra; *Special Verses Collected by Topic, (Udānavarga; Ched du brjod pa'i tshoms)* compiled by Dharmatrāta; *Compendium of Trainings, (Shikṣhāsamuchchayakārikā; bsLab pa kun las btus pa'i tsig le'ur byas pa) and Guide to the Bodhisattva's Way of Life, (Bodhisattvacharyāvatāra; Byang chub sems dpa'i spyod pa la 'jug pa)* by Shāntideva.

11. Lang (gLang) and Nyö (gNyos) from Nyal (gNyal), Ram and Nang (sNang) from Tsang, Ja (Bya) and Phag from Kham, 'Be and Rog from Dolpo, Lang (gLang-ri-gtang-pa) and Shar (Shar-ra-ba), Geshey Drab-pa (Grab-pa), Geshey Ding-pa (lDing-pa), and the great Drag-kar (Brag-dkar).
12. Zhan-tön (Zhan-gton) Sha-ra-wa
13. Chö-lung Ku-sheg (Chos-lung sku-gshegs), Tab-ka-wa (sTabs-ka-ba), Nyi-mel-dul-wa-dzin-pa (Nyi-mal-'dul-ba-'dzin-pa) and the great Che-ka-wa (Chad-kha-ba).
14. Nyel-chag-zhing-pa (gNyal-lcags-żhing-pa)
15. The yogi Jang-seng (Byang-seng) of Dro-sa (Gro-sa), the meditator Jang-ye (Byang-ye) from Ren-tsa-rab (Ran-tsa-rab), Gen-pa-ton-dar (Gan-pa-ston-dar) of Ba-lam, the all-knowing master Lho-pa, Gya-pang Sa-thaṇg-pa (brGya-spang-thang-pa), the great teacher Ram-pa Lha-ding-pa (Ram-pa-lha-sdings-pa), and the unequalled master Gyal-wa-se (rGyal-ba-se).
16. Lha-chen-po Lung-gi-wang-chug (Lha-chen-po Lung-gi-dbang-phyug)
17. Sha-kya So-nam Gyel-tsen Pel-zang-po (Sa-kya bSod-nams rGyal-mtsan dPal-bzang-po).
18. Thog-me Zang-po (Thogs-med bZang-po).
19. Kyab-chog Pal-zang-po (sKyabs-mchog dPal-bzang-po)
20. Nāgas are beings sometimes classed as animals sometimes as spirits, who dwell in or near ponds, rivers, water-sources or trees and are commonly associated with the fertility of the land, but who can also function as protectors of religion.
21. Buddhist cosmology divides the world into four continents, of which this world is the southern continent. This may have initially referred to India the original home of Buddhism, which is the southernmost continent of the Asian landmass. Extending the definition to include the entire known world serves to include all human beings of his planet in the fortunate class of those capable of practising Buddhism, but gives rise to a problem about where the other four continents are located.
22. The lifespan of the beings of the northern world is definite.
23. Shakra is an epithet in Buddhist literature for Indra King of the Gods.
24. Dharani—retention mantra.
25. Nāgārjuna, Shāntideva and Asaṅga.
26. The misconception that the self is inherently existent, existent by way of its own characteristics and so forth.
27. In Tibet tea came in the form of a compressed brick and you would chop or shave off a little whenever you wanted to brew tea.
28. The eight hot hells are the reviving hell, the black line hell, the capturing and annihilation hell, the wailing, the great wailing, the hot, the very hot and the unceasing hells.
29. The eight cold hells are the blistering, that of bursting blisters, the

sneezing, the coughing, the teeth-grating, the shattering like a blue lotus, the shattering like a red lotus and the shattering like a gigantic lotus hells.

30. The surrounding hells are for example the plain of fire, the putrid swamp, and the forest of knives.
31. The seven jewels of an exalted being are: confidence in the law of cause and effect, ethical discipline, generosity, listening to teachings, a sense of shame, consideration for others, and intelligent awareness discriminating between meaningful and meaningless actions.
32. The seven good qualities of high status are: long life, magnificent form and personality, belonging to a noble family, being prosperous and influential, being readily believed by others, having great power, and having a strong body and a courageous mind.
33. The perfect body of truth - *dharmakaya; chos-sku.*
34. In Buddhist cosmology the world is divided into the four main and the eight sub-continents, of which we live on the southern continent—see n.21 above.
35. The various classes of gods mentioned here are listed in full in *Meditative States* by Lati Rinbochay, Denma Lochö Rinbochay, Leah Zahler & Jeffrey Hopkins (London, Wisdom, 1983).
36. The three dairy products are milk, butter and curd.
37. The three sweets are white sugar, brown sugar and honey.
38. Akya Yongzin says 'the seven generations' refers to the idea that those within seven generations are our relatives, which we assume only through the force of preconceptions.
39. The image of heaps of black hair trimmings would have been easily understood in Tibet, because whenever a monk or nun had their head shaved, clumps of such trimmings or shavings would fall in heaps around them.
40. In the classic Buddhist explanation beings consist of a combination of body and mind described as the five mental and physical aggregates: form (which in general terms refers to the body), feelings, discriminations, compositional factors, and consciousness.
41. The six causes and one result training in the awakening mind consists of: 1. recognition that all beings have at one time been your mother; 2. recognition of their kindness; 3. the wish to repay that kindness; 4. love (the wish for all beings to be happy); 5. compassion (the wish for all beings to be free from suffering); 6. the special wish - the determination to fulfil these wishes yourself; and, the result, which is the awakening mind.
42. A story is told in the sutras of a Bhikshu who was attached to his alms bowl when he died. As a result he was almost immediately reborn as a worm in the bowl and was overwhelmed by the fire of anger. At the

time the Bhikṣhu's body was cremated the worm died and was reborn in one of the hot hells. Thus, it was said that, due to attachment, the Bhikṣhu burned thrice simultaneously.

43. This apt translation belongs to Ken McLeod. The Tibetan says, 'Don't put the dzo's load on an ox.' The dzo, a cross between a yak and a cow, is much stronger than an ox and so is able to carry much more.
44. The Tibetan idiom here refers to a relationship so close that not even a dog could come between you.
45. *rig pa; vidya*
46. *shes rab; prajña*
47. The four seals are:
    i. All composite phenomena are transitory,
    ii. All contaminated things are miserable,
    iii. All phenomena have no self-existence,
    iv. Nirvana, the state beyond sorrow, is peace.
48. *sems tsams pa; Chittamātra*
49. *dbu ma pa; Mādhyamika*
50. *thal gyur pa; Prāsaṅgika*
51. *rang rgyud pa; Svātantrika*
52. *bye brag smra ba; Vaibhāṣhika*
53. *mdo sde pa; Sautrāntika*
54. The 'mind basis of all' consciousness; *kun gzhi rnam par shes pa; ālayavijñāna*
55. There are different types of distorted cognition. If a cognition is distorted with regard to the object that appears to it, it is not necessarily wrong. However, if it is distorted with regard to its referent object it is always wrong. For instance, mentally holding a vase to be truly existent is distorted with regard to its referent object - the actual nature of the vase—because the vase is not truly existent. For a consciousness to be distorted with regard to the object that appears to it take the example of a vase devoid of true existence. Here the consciousness perceives its referent object without distortion, because it is an inferential valid cognition. The object which appears in this case will be a mental image of the emptiness of the vase. This is distorted with regard to the object appearing to it, because the mental image of the emptiness of the vase is held to be its emptiness.
56. *Gandharvas; dri zha*, literally 'scent-eaters' are phantom-like celestial musicians, their mythical city is a traditional example of illusoriness.
57. This heading is not mentioned specifically in the text, but is implied by the main heading above it.
58. This heading is placed as a subheading of How to Determine the Selfless of Persons because that is the position it occupies in the text. However, the discussion of analytical meditation here deals with establishing the selflessness of persons and phenomena.

59. Although not explicitly mentioned in the text this heading is implied by the two which follow it and which are referred to as second and third.
60. This heading is labelled (i) because of its position in the actual explanation, although it is actually marked 'second'. That refers to the second heading concerning meditative techniques, of which this refers to formal meditation, but also concerns the selflessness of both persons and phenomena.

BIBLIOGRAPHY

Sutras and Tantras

Adornment of Mañjushrī's Realm Sutra
Ārya Mañjushrībuddhakṣhetregaṇavyūhasūtra
'Phags pa 'jam dpal gyi sangs rgyas kyi shing gi yon tan bkod pa'i mdo
P760.15, Vol. 23

Array of Tree-trunks Sutra
Ghandhavyūhasūtra
sDong pos rgyan pa
P761.45, Vol. 26

Biography of Manibhadra
Manibhadravimoksha
Nor bzangs kyis dge ba'i bshes gnyen bsnyen bkur ba
P761.(45), Vol. 26

Buddhāvataṃsaka Sutra
Buddhāvatamsakanāmamahāvaipulyasūtra
Sangs rgyas phal po che zhes bya ba shin tu rgyas pa chen po mdo
P761, Vol. 25-6

Cloud of Jewels Sutra
Ratnameghasūtra
dKon mchog sprin gyi mdo
P879, Vol. 35

Compendium of Perfect Doctrine Sutra
Dharmasaṃgītisūtra
Chos yang dag par sdud pa'i mdo
P904, Vol. 36

Condensed Perfection of Wisdom Sutra
Sañchayagāthāprajñāpāramitāsūtra
Shes rab kyi pha rol tu phyin pa sdud pa tshigs su bchad pa
P735, Vol. 21

Entering into the Womb Sutra
Āyuṣhmanandagarbhāvakrāntisūtra
dGa' bo mngal na 'jug pa'i mdo
P760.13, Vol. 23

Expression of the Names of Mañjushrī
Mañjushrīnāmasaṃgīti
'Jam dpal mtshan brjod
P2, Vol. 1

Extensive Sport Sutra
Lalitavistarasūtra
rGya cher rol pa'i mdo
P763, Vol.27
English translation (from the French) by Gwendolyn Bays, *The Lalitavistara Sūtra: The Voice of the Buddha, the Beauty of Compassion* (Berkeley: Dharma Publishing, 1983)

King of Meditative Stabilisation Sutra
Samādhirājasūtra
Ting nge 'dzin rgyal po'i mdo
P795, Vol. 31-2
Partial translation by K. Regamey, *Three Chapters from the Samādhirājasūtra* (Warsaw: 1938)

Life-story of the Exalted Maitreya
Aryamaitreyavimoksha
Phags pa'i byams pa'i rnam pa thar pa
(?) P761, Vol. 25-6

Prayers of the Meditator Vidyujjvāla
Vidyujjvālasamādhipraṇidhāna (?)
sGom pa glog 'bar gyi smon lam

Questions of Gaganagañja Sutra
Gaganagañjaparipṛcchanāmamahāyānasūtra
Nam mkha' mdzod kyis zhus pa'i mdo
P815, Vol.

Questions of Anavatapta, the King of the Nāgas, Sutra
Anavataptanāgarājaparipṛcchāsūtra
kLu'i rgyal po ma dros pas zhur pa'i mdo
P823, Vol. 33

Questions of Subāhu Sutra
Subāhuparipṛchchānāmasūtra
Lag bzang gis zhus pa'i mdo
P428, Vol. 9

Questions of Upāli Sutra
Vinayavinishcayaupāliparipṛcchāsūtra
'Dul ba rnam par gtan la dbab pa nye bar 'khor gyis zhus pa'i mdo
P760.24, Vol. 24?

Questions of Viradutta Sutra
Viraduttagṛhapatiparipṛcchāsūtra
Khyim bdag dpas byin gyis zhus pa'i mdo
P760.28, Vol. 28?

Sutra of Advice for a King
Rājadeshanāmamahāyānasūtra
rGyal po la gdams pa'i mdo
P880, Vol. 35

Sutra of the Vajra Victory Banner
Vajradvājaparipranitsūtra (?)
rDo rje rgyal tshan gyi yongs su bsngo ba
P761.30, Vol. 25

Sutra on Avoiding Sorrow
Shokavinodana
Mya ngan bsal ba
P5418, Vol. 103 /P5677, Vol. 129

Transmission of Discipline
Vinayāgāma
'Dul ba lung
P1045, Vol. 45

Vajrapāni Initiation Tantra
Vajrapāṇyabhiṣhekamahātantra
Lak na rdo rje dbang bskur ba'i rgyud chen mo
P130, Vol. 6

SANSKRIT AND TIBETAN TREATISES

Āryadeva

Four Hundred Verses
Chatuḥshatakashāstrakārikā
bsTan bcos bzhi brgya pa zhes bya ba'i tshig le'ur byas pa
P5246, Vol. 95
Translated by Geshe Sonam Rinchen and Ruth Sonam, *The Four Hundred Stanzas on the Yogic Deeds of Bodhisattvas* (Ithaca, NY: Snowlion, forthcoming)

Āryashūra

Birth Stories
Jātakamālā
sKyes pa'i rabs kyi rgyud
P5650, Vol.128
Translation by J.S. Speyer, *The Jātakamālā - Garland of Birth Stories of Āryaśūra* (First published 1895; reprinted Delhi: Motilal Banarsidass, 1971)

Asaṅga

Spiritual Stages of a Bodhisattva
Yogacharyābhūmau Bodhisattvabhūmi
rNal 'byor spyod pa'i sa las byang chub sems dpa'i sa
P5538, Vol. 110

Bhāvaviveka

Blaze of Reasoning
Madhyamakahṛdayavṛttitarkajvālā
dbu ma snying po'i 'grel pa rtog ge bar ba
P5256, Vol. 96
Partial translation by S. Iida in *Reason and Emptiness* (Tokyo: Hokuseido, 1980), chap. III. 1-136, pp.52-242

Chandrakīrti

Commentary to (Aryadeva's) 'Four Hundred Verses on the Yogic Deeds of Bodhisattvas'

Bodhisattvayogacharyāchatuḥshatakaṭikā
Byang chub sems dpa'i rnal 'byor spyod pa bzhi brgya pa'i rgya cher 'grel pa
P5266, Vol.98

Supplement to (Nagarjuna's) 'Treatise on the Middle Way'
Madhyamakāvatāra
dbu ma la 'jug pa
P5261, Vol. 98; P5262, Vol. 98
English translation (Ch.I-V), Jeffrey Hopkins, in *Compassion in Tibetan Buddhism* (Valois, NY: Gabriel Snow Lion, 1980) and (Ch.VI), Stephen Batchelor, trans. in *Echoes of Voidness* by Geshe Rabten (London: Wisdom, 1983)

Dharmakīrti
Commentary on (Dignāga's) 'Compendium of Valid Cognition'
Pramāṇavarttikakārikā
Tshad ma rnam 'grel gyi tshig le'ur byas pa
P5709, Vol. 130

Dharmatrāta
Special Verses Collected by Topic
Udānavarga
Ched du brjod pa'i tshoms
P5600, Vol. 119
Translation with introduction by Gareth Sparham et al, *The Tibetan Dhammapada-Sayings of the Buddha* (Rev. ed. London: Wisdom, 1986)

Jagatamitrānanda
Letter to Chandraraja
Candrarājalekha
rGyal po zla ba la springs pa'i 'phrin yig
P5689 Vol. 129

Kamalashīla
Stages of Meditation
Bhāvanākrama
sGom pa'i rim pa
P5310-12, Vol. 102

Lang-ri Thang-pa
Eight Verses for Training the Mind
bLo sbyong tshig brgyad ma in *bLo sbyong brgya rtsa* (Dharamsala:

Tibetan Cultural Printing Press, 1973)
Translation with commentary by H.H. the Dalai Lạma in *Kindness, Clarity and Insight* (Ithaca, NY: Snow Lion, 1984) and in *Four Essential Buddhist Commentaries* (Dharamsala: LTWA, 1982)

Maitreya
Discrimination of the Middle Way and the Extremes
Madhyāntavibhaṅga
dbUs dang mtha' rnam par 'byed pa
P5522, Vol. 108
Translated in part by T. Scherbatsky, *Madhyānta-Vibhanga* (Calcutta: Indian Studies Past and Present, 1971)

Ornament for Clear Realisation
Abhisamayālaṃkāra
mNgon par rtogs pa'i rgyan
P5184, Vol. 88
Translated by E. Conze, *Abhisamayālamkāra*, Serie Orientale Roma VI (Rome: I.S.M.E.O., July 1954)

Ornament for Great Vehicle Sutras
Mahāyānasūtralaṃkārakārikā
Theg pa chen po'i mdo sde'i rgyan gyi tshig le'ur byas pa
P5521, Vol. 108

Mātṛceta / Māticitra
Letter to Kanika
Mahārājakanikalekha
rGyal po chen po ka ni ka la spring pa'i 'phrin yig
P5684 Vol. 129

Praise of the Praiseworthy
Varṇārhavarṇebhagavatebuddhasyastotrashakyastaranāma
bsNgags par 'os pa bsngags pa las bstod par mi nus par bstod pa shes bya ba
P2029, Vol. 46

Nāgārjuna
Commentary on the Awakening Mind
Bodhichittavaraṇa
Byang chub sems kyi 'grel pa
P2665, Vol. 61; P2666, Vol. 61

Friendly Letter
Suhṛllekha
bShes pa'i spring yig
P5682, Vol. 129
Translation by Geshe L. Tharchin and A.B. Engle, *Nāgārjuna's Letter* (Dharamsala: LTWA, 1979), and *Nāgārjuna's Letter to King Gautamiputra* by Ven. Lozang Jamspal, Ven. Ngawang Samten Chophel and Peter Della Santina (Delhi: Motilal Barnasidass, 1978)

Fundamental Treatise on the Middle Way, Called 'Wisdom'
Prajñānāmamūlamadhyamakakārikā
dbU ma rtsa pa'i tshig le'ur byas pa shes rab ces bya ba
P5224, Vol. 95
Translated by F.J. Streng, *Emptiness - A Study in Religious Meaning* (Nashville and New York: Abingdon, 1967)

Precious Garland (of Advice for a King)
Rājaparikathāratnāvalī
rGyal po la gtam bya ba rin po che'i phreng ba
P5658, Vol. 129
Translated by J. Hopkins and Lati Rinpoche in *The Precious Garland and The Song of the Four Mindfulnesses.* (London: George Allen and Unwin, 1975)

Seventy Stanzas on Emptinesses
Shūnyatāsaptatikārikā
sTong pa nyid bdun cu pa'i tshig le'ur byas pa
P5227, Vol. 95
Translation in *Nāgārjuna's Seventy Stanzas: A Buddhist Psychology of Emptiness* by David Ross Komito with Geshe Sonam Rinchen and Tenzin Dorjee (Ithaca, NY: Snow Lion, 1987)

Sixty Stanzas of Reasoning
Yuktiṣhaṣhṭikākārikā
Rigs pa drug cu pa'i tshig le'ur byas pa
P5225, Vol. 95

Parahitaghoṣha Āraṇyaka
Seventy Prayers
Praṇidhānasaptatināmagāthā
sMon lam bdun cu pa shes bya ba'i tshigs su bcad pa
P5430, Vol. 103 / P5936, Vol. 150

Potowa
Teachings by Example
Po to ba'i dpe chos rin chen spungs pa
(Sarnath: Mongolian Lama Gurudev, 1965)

Prayers of Supreme Conduct
Agracharyāpraṇidhāna
mChog gi spyod pa'i smon lam
P718, Vol. 11 / P5939, Vol. 150

Prayers for Granting Supreme Love
Āryamaitrīpraṇidhāna
'Phags pa'i byams pa smon lam
P717, Vol. 11 / P5925, Vol. 150

Shāntideva
Compendium of Trainings
Shikṣhāsamuchchayakārikā
bsLab pa kun las btus pa'i tsig le'ur byas pa
P5336, Vol. 102
Translated by C. Bendall and W.H.D. Rouse, *Śikṣā Samuccaya* (Delhi: Motilal Banarsidass, 1971)

Guide to the Bodhisattva's Way of Life
Bodhisattvacharyāvatāra
Byang chub sems dpa'i spyod pa la 'jug pa
P5272, Vol. 99
Translated by Stephen Batchelor, *A Guide to the Bodhisattva's Way of Life* (Dharamsala: LTWA, 1979)

Tsong-kha-pa
Great Exposition of the Stages of the Path
sKyes bu gsum gyi nyams su blang ba'i rim pa thams cad tshan bar ston pa'i byang chub lam gyi rim pa (Lam rim chen mo) P6001, Vol. 152

Udbhaṭasiddhasvāmin
Especially Exalted Praise
Visheshastava
Khyad par du 'phags pa'i bstod pa
P2001, Vol. 46

Vasubandhu
Treasury of Knowledge
Abhidharmakoshakarika
Chos ngon pa'i mdzod kyi tshig le'ur byas pa
P5590, Vol.115

OTHER RELATED WORKS

Conze, Edward tr.
The Perfection of Wisdom in Eight Thousand Lines and its verse commentary (Bolinas: Four Seasons Foundation, 1973).

Dalai Lama, H.H. the
Four Essential Buddhist Commentaries including commentaries on *Eight Verses on the Training of the Mind* and *Thirty-seven Bodhisattva Practices* (Dharamsala: LTWA, 1982)

Dhargyey, Geshe Ngawang,
Anthology of Well-spoken Advice: on the graded paths of the mind ed. Alex Berzin, tr. Sharpa Tulku (Dharamsala: LTWA, 1982)

Dharmarakshita
Wheel of Sharp Weapons tr. and comm. Geshe Ngawang Dhargyey et al., (Dharamsala: LTWA, 1974, 1982)

Gyatso, Tenzin, the Fourteenth Dalai Lama
Opening the Mind and Generating a Good Heart tr. Tsepak Rigzin & Jeremy Russell (Dharamsala: LTWA, 1985)

Gyatso, Geshe Kelsang
Universal Compassion (London: Tharpa, 1988)

Gyeltsen, Geshe Tsultim
Keys to Great Enlightenment (commentaries on *Eight Verses of Thought Training and The Thirty-seven Bodhisattva Practices*) (Los Angeles: Thubten Dhargye Ling, 1989)

Hopkins, Jeffrey
Meditation on Emptiness (London: Wisdom, 1983)

Kongtrul, Jamgon
The Great Path of Awakening tr. Ken McLeod (Boston: Shambhala, 1987)

Napper, Elizabeth
Dependent Arising and Emptiness (London: Wisdom, 1989)

Rabten, Geshe & Dhargyey, Geshe Ngawang
Advice from a Spiritual Friend (London: Wisdom, 1984)